RETURN TO AUSCHWITZ

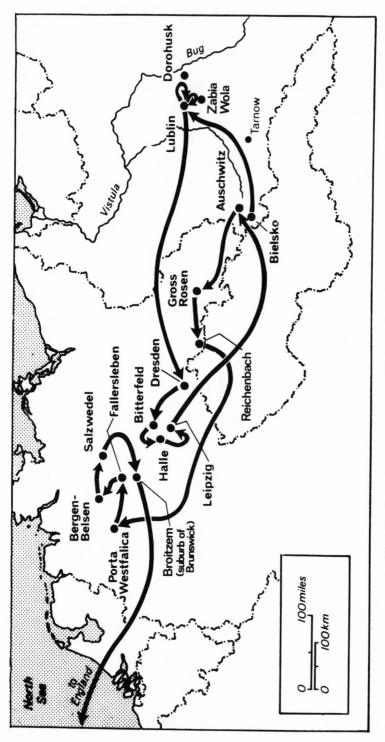

Kitty Hart's wartime journeys: from Bielsko, where she was born, to Lublin and then to Dorohusk, where she and her family tried in vain to cross into the Soviet Union; back to the Lublin ghetto and then to prison in Germany; then to Auschwitz, where she and her mother spent nearly twenty months, and finally, after a series of camps, to England

Return to Auschwitz

The remarkable story of
a girl who survived
the Holocaust

KITTY HART

ATHENEUM   NEW YORK

1982

Library of Congress Cataloging in Publication Data

Hart, Kitty.
    Return to Auschwitz.
    Includes index.
    1. Auschwitz (Poland: Concentration camp)
2. Holocaust, Jewish (1939-1945)—Poland—Personal
narratives. 3. Hart, Kitty. I. Title.
D805.P7H37 1982   940.53′15′03924   81-69155
ISBN 0-689-11266-1   AACR2

Manufactured by American Book-Stratford Press,
Saddle Brook, New Jersey
First Printing February 1982
Second Printing May 1982

In memory of
my mother,
without whose love and devotion
I would have perished long ago

Acknowledgements

I AM grateful to many friends who have encouraged and helped me in the preparation of this book. First I must thank John Burke, whose patient questioning and argument drew out of me so many things I thought I had forgotten, and who worked closely with me over several months sorting these out into what we both hope is the right order.

Then there has been, as ever, the support of my family: Ralph, David and Peter. Also I owe a special debt to Philip Moxon for sparing me from other duties and for offering so much practical advice and comment throughout.

Yorkshire Television not only produced what I found to be a sympathetic, evocative interpretation of what I had to tell them, but since transmission of their programme have continued to provide help in any number of ways and have agreed to my using whatever I needed from their scripts and research material. In particular I should most warmly mention Paul Fox, Peter Morley, Kevin Sim, Frank Pocklington, Barbara Twigg, Michael Crossley and Jane Stewart.

Martin Gilbert gave generously of his time to advise on illustrations and other aspects, and allowed the use of his own map outlining the course of my travels. Erich Kulka was equally ready to help with photographs: the illustration of Himmler and Rudolf Höss is from his own collection, now in the possession of Yad Vashem in Jerusalem, and he provided the plan of Birkenau.

I am also grateful to Yad Vashem and the Auschwitz Museum for supplying illustrations, with particular thanks to Tadeusz Szymanski for the personal trouble he took in the Auschwitz Archives on my behalf and in having the picture of the lavatory block specially photographed for me.

Kitty Hart
Birmingham, February 1981

Contents

Illustrations

RETURN TO AUSCHWITZ

I

The Promised Land

I WAS so excited that September day in 1946 when I saw the white cliffs of Dover for the first time. Mother and I were crying with happiness. We had been close to death so many times – in the ghetto, on the run, in Auschwitz with its gas chambers and ovens – and might so easily not have lived to reach these shores.

'It's going to be all right now,' my mother kept telling me. 'You'll be able to go to school again, and you'll soon catch up. Everything's going to be wonderful. Oh, you'll love England.'

I was only too ready to love England. Mother had talked such a lot about it. Studying at Bedford College, she had been in London at the time of King George V's coronation, and had never forgotten it. Back home in Poland she taught English up to state examination level, and also ran her own little nursery school, where a great deal of English was spoken and sung.

In 1939 her sister and brother-in-law, threatened by the anti-Jewish terrorism which increased after Hitler's seizure of Austria, fled from Vienna and settled in Birmingham. Now that we were coming to join them they would look after us and would surely know the best place for me to go to school. With a little extra tuition in English I would soon be able to cope with other subjects.

Looking back, I think what makes me most bitter against the Nazis, even after all this time, is the education of which they robbed me. I've tried to make up the lost ground, but those lost years were never fully compensated for.

Things didn't work out at all as Mother had predicted.

My uncle was waiting at Dover. The moment we got into his car he staggered us by saying firmly: 'Before we go off to Birmingham there's one thing I must make quite clear. On no account are you to talk about any of the things that have happened to you. Not in my house. I don't want my girls upset. And *I* don't want to know.'

I was soon to discover that everybody in England would be talking about personal war experiences for months, even years, after hostilities had ceased. But we, who had been pursued over Europe by the mutual enemy, and come close to extermination at the hands of that enemy, were not supposed to embarrass people by saying a word.

We spent our first night in London, and my uncle showed us round. It was bewildering. I had not seen an undamaged house or tidy streets for years. A well-lit shop was something unknown. And shops like *these* . . . department stores . . . and all that food! I didn't want to be hurried along sight-seeing, but just to stand and gape.

This brief treat over, we travelled next day to Birmingham. Here I was utterly at a loss. My cousins Susie and Eva, girls close to my own age, never questioned me about the past; and I was forbidden to mention of my own accord any of the things which had dominated my life these last seven years. The two girls were uncomfortable when I tagged along, and unsure how to explain me to their friends. Left to myself, I wandered along one street after another, simply looking. Susie then lent me her bicycle so that I could go a bit faster and further. Looking was all I could do. We had come to England with nothing, and my uncle never thought to offer me even a few pence pocket money.

I waited for someone to make a suggestion regarding my future. Above all I was keen on two things: going back to school, and taking up physical training again – I had once represented Poland in the Youth Swimming Team against Hungary, and had proudly finished up with a bronze medal.

But my uncle dashed all hopes of my going to school. 'Who'd pay for it?' I was nineteen and it was time I found somewhere to live and some way of supporting myself.

Although my mother and I had come to England on special permits and our fares had been paid by U.N.R.R.A. (United Nations Relief and Rehabilitation Administration) we found ourselves in many ways worse off than apparently less favoured refugees. Those without homes, families or contacts were offered generous help in resettlement. We two, being supposedly under the wing of a relative who had vouched for us, could get no assistance at all.

My permit prohibited permanent employment but somehow Aunt Olga got round this and arranged for me to start on a nurse's training course. In Vienna before the war she had been a well-known children's dentist, and had also studied medicine. On reaching England she was accepted as a doctor in the Accident Hospital and worked there until her retirement at the age of eighty. Now I was to start at the bottom in that same hospital. As for my mother, there was no opening for a Pole to teach English to the English, so she became housekeeper to a very pleasant, kindly widower. He was planning to go to Australia, offered to take her with him, and asked her to marry him. But she didn't want to be uprooted yet again.

Life in the nurses' home made me feel more outlandish than ever. In such surroundings there was no way of concealing the tattoo on my forearm. Some days when I felt very low I would cover it with sticking plaster. On others I would defiantly let it be seen. People stared, but only occasionally asked questions. Was it a laundry mark? Or a boy-friend's telephone number? Rashly I answered a couple of times with the truth: that it was my concentration camp number. The reaction was always an awkward silence, as if I had said something terribly ill mannered.

On 5 November one of the girls took me along to a Bonfire Night party. I hadn't been given any idea what to expect, and was horrified by the huge pyre, the flames and smoke, and the effigy of Guy Fawkes. 'I'm sorry,' I wept, 'I can't stand it. The smoke . . . I can't tell you.' For me there was not merely flame and smoke and that burning figure, but the memory of an awful smell hanging over it all. I fumbled out some sort of explanation about the fires and the stench of roasting meat coming from human beings in the Auschwitz ovens. My companion didn't believe a word of it, and obviously thought I was quite mad.

One hope lingered. Because our translating work had been done for both American and British liberation forces, we had been granted entry permits for both countries. At first I had wanted to go to the United States; but my mother favoured England because of past associations and the thought of our relatives already there. The decisive factor for me, in the end, was a man.

Sex was something I'd had little chance of learning about before I was sent to the ghetto and then to the extermination camp. In that camp, where any attempt by a man and a woman to get together was punishable by instant death, chances for communication were few. Not until I found myself in a Displaced Persons camp earlier in this year of 1946 was I introduced to the gentler pleasures of sex, and then by a young Englishman working with a Quaker relief team. He returned to England before permits for my mother and myself came through, but we started writing to each other and I was sure we could sort out some way of being happy. Now, from Birmingham, I turned to him.

What I did not discover until later was that his return to England from the D.P. camp had not been just a routine transfer. His father held an important position in their local community, was anxious for his son to resume the university course which he had given up in order to work with the relief team, and equally anxious for him to marry into their own class of people. Alarmed by what his son told him about me, he arranged a meeting with my uncle and aunt. At the same time he summoned the young man home and insisted on his returning to university. Now when we met in England we both knew things had changed. This world was so different from the one we had briefly inhabited in Germany. He realized it sooner than I did, and finally broke off our relationship – in a letter.

It may seem grotesque to say, after surviving the tortures and terrors of Auschwitz, that this was one of the unhappiest times of my life. But for such a long time I had been forcing myself to hold on, had refused to give in, had kept going in the assurance that there *had* to be light at the end of the tunnel. And still there was no light. Of course there were no longer the raving bullies ready at every minute of the day and night to beat one to death with whips and cudgels. But even in the outside world there are so many different ways of beating people to their knees. This was the nearest I ever came to total despair.

The hospital and the nurses' home grew more and more unfriendly. With my background, perhaps I was not the right sort of person to work there. Patients in some of the wards looked so comfortable in their nice clean beds, and quite fit by the standards of what I had been seeing over recent years. How could I feel the proper sympathy for them? Once I tried to confide in a sister who was harassing me, who didn't like the way I did this or didn't do that, who was sure I was not putting my heart into my work. 'But I've seen people dying, you just don't know, *they're* not ill in there, if you'd seen people dying by the thousand the way I've seen them . . .' It was a mistake. What I said made no sense to her or anyone else.

From their point of view I must have seemed an alien creature. It was difficult for me to be polite and deferential. In the world of the concentration camp there had been no courtesies. You fought for everything. If you lost, you cursed. Curses and blows were more common than even the slightest nod of friendship. Illness had to be very serious indeed before anyone paid any attention: and when it did get that serious, it usually meant instant despatch to the incinerators. From a world of ceaseless bullying and shouting, of beatings and hunger and hatred, it was hard to adjust to artificial politeness, manners and mannerisms.

Not so long ago I'd had to scheme, battle or barter for a crust, and eat it with my fingers, if someone else didn't snatch it away. Now, in the dining room, everything was so formal. Matron sat above us in state; the sisters were arrayed below her. Grace was solemnly said. Correct behaviour was essential. I watched every little movement of the others, the way they used their knives and forks – while they, in turn, watched me. I wanted to break out, disobey, be done with all their petty rituals and hypocrisy, above all to be free from the sister who made it so plain that nothing I did was right or ever would be. 'You'll have to go.' It was her constant refrain. 'You'll have to go.'

Very well then, I would go. I told my uncle and aunt that I just couldn't carry on. They were as incapable as the hospital staff of under-standing what I was talking about. The only thing they could think of doing was to send me off to see a psychiatrist in the hope that he would find out why I was so difficult and had such silly notions, especially about going to school and getting a proper education. I must admit I was peevishly ready to encounter yet another persecutor, but in fact the psychiatrist turned out to be a charming, sympathetic man. After listening to everything I had to say, he came out with the opinion that I was absolutely right: there was nothing much wrong with me, but a lot wrong with the other people concerned. He didn't get me out of my nurses' training, but he did, in the shrewdest and most helpful way, give me encouragement.

By now my mother had found another post as housekeeper, this time with the family of a prosperous businessman who invited her to spend Christmas with them on the Welsh coast. My uncle, aunt and cousins also planned to be away over the holiday. I had taken it for granted that I would be in the hospital over Christmas, but I was given four days' leave and told only at the last minute that this meant vacating my room. Where was I to go?

During training I received no payment other than a very small allow-ance of pocket money. All my belongings would go into one small case. So I took this and set off, not knowing where I was going to sleep. Even if I'd had enough money, I knew nothing about such things as hotels.

How naive I was in those days! I never dreamt of going to the authorities and explaining my predicament. Over recent years I had learned never to approach authorities. To go near anyone in a position of power in a concentration camp was to invite at the very least a savage beating, and more likely an immediate death sentence. You didn't ask questions or complain: you had to find your own way of surviving. I had grown accustomed to handling danger almost with ease, or at least without being *too* frightened. But the pitfalls of every-day life in a foreign land were unfamiliar ground. I didn't know the rules, or whether they were good or bad rules, or how to go along with them or get round them. It was a whole new game; and not one single person had so much as noticed that I needed a bit of instruction in the simplest opening moves.

In the end the waiting-room of Snow Hill railway station became my bedroom for three nights. It was packed when I got there. People were coming and going the whole of that first evening. Then it began to empty, leaving a collection of drunks and some other odd types who didn't seem to have much idea where they were or where they were supposed to go next. But the place was warm and cosy enough. I'd known worse: my God, had I known worse! With less than £1 on me, I bought some bread and something to drink, trusting the change would spin out over the holiday. It hadn't occurred to me that on Christmas Day there would be absolutely nowhere open to buy any food.

Boxing Day was spent walking all over the town and out into the suburbs. Somewhere children were singing carols. In the early twilight lights went on in people's windows, and families gathered round their tables. It was just like all the sentimental pictures you've ever seen, and all the sad fairy-tales you've ever read. Only for me it was real. Even now the memory makes me feel like crying.

Tired out, I returned to the waiting-room and settled down on a bench. A few tramps spent the night there too in the warm. Next morning a wash in the ladies' toilet, then off to wander the streets again. I ventured into front gardens, peering into windows, scuttling away if anyone glanced out. What hurt most was that nobody, anywhere, cared about me. I couldn't blame those who didn't even know I existed. But others did know I existed, and *they* hadn't cared: so wrapped up in their own Christmas holiday preparations that they just couldn't be bothered. Never one for self-pity, I was close to it then; tears streamed down my face. But I was free, no longer a prisoner, nobody was going to come round the next corner and whip me towards the gas chamber, so why the tears?

I was learning what loneliness meant. In the ghetto and the concentration camp, in the Displaced Persons camp and recently in the hospital, there were always people around. Overcrowded conditions, maybe, but not lonely.

A family of my own – that was what I must build. A home and a family. So much of my earlier family had been destroyed: now I had to make another so that never again would I have to walk streets utterly alone.

Soon after this I left the hospital for good. It hadn't crossed my mind that I was supposed to give a month's notice before doing such a shocking thing, and undoubtedly my name must have been in worse odour than before. But at that moment I was ready to go back to Germany, back to the D.P. camp where I still had friends, and start all over again. Yet how could I leave my mother? We had stuck together through the worst days and nights, and there was a very special relationship between us. We were not really like mother and daughter at all. I don't mean, as some might put it, that we were more like sisters. It was something quite different, very hard to explain to anyone else. When only thirteen or fourteen I had virtually had to look after her; at other times she had sustained me; and each had saved the other's life more than once. Sometimes we found difficulty in expressing ourselves, and sometimes argued and didn't get on at all. But even in our disagreements it was something quite other than a mother and daughter squabbling. Unthinkable for us to go separate ways now; and just as unthinkable for me to coax her into returning to the camp with me.

I went to London and stayed with a Quaker friend, Jane, who made me tell her everything and urged me to seek a job for which I was better fitted. But how could one be fitted for any job without at least a basic English education? We approached the Jewish community to see if they could help, only to be told that there were no funds for people like me. They were generous when it came to collecting secondhand clothes and sending them to the Continent, but a batch of old clothes was not what I needed. I wanted help there and then, and would gladly have come to any arrangement to pay it back in due course. There was nothing doing. Cast-off garments from the past, yes; help for the future, no.

While in the Accident Hospital I had been fascinated by the imposing X-ray machinery. With my interest in sport and gymnastics, physiotherapy seemed to be my line, but there again one needed money for training. I wondered if there was any way I could possibly study radiography without having to find fees.

Often I had noticed a distinguished-looking man going in and out of the X-ray room, and discovered he was the eminent Dr James Brailsford. I plucked up the courage to approach him. Again my behaviour was unorthodox. Having looked up his address, but with no idea of making an appointment or anything like that, I simply took a bus out to Edgbaston and showed up on his doorstep. His receptionist was very chilly. No, I made it clear, I was not a patient but it was essential for me to see Dr Brailsford. Maybe my bad English and foreign accent made the receptionist more sympathetic, or perhaps less sure of herself, than she would have been with anyone else trying to force their way in. She showed me into the waiting-room, and after a while Dr Brailsford came out. He looked me up and down without much enthusiasm.

'I wish a word with you, sir.' It was the best I could manage. 'Please, I do wish to have a word with you.'

After a moment's hesitation he took me into his consulting room. I sat down, and all at once it began to come out, all of it. In what must then have been the most awful sort of blundering English I told him how I had seen him in the corridors of the hospital, how I admired the wonderful machines I had seen, how I wanted to do something useful but was not cut out for nursing, and how I'd had this idea that he might do something for me or tell me who could do something.

'And here I am.' I remember to this day how I just said that and then sat there feeling helpless.

He did his best to put me at ease. He asked where I had come from, and what I was doing in Birmingham. I told him I couldn't express myself very well in English, and couldn't read and write it very well either. But I tried to give him an outline of all that had gone on in recent years. I shall never forget the patience with which he listened to me, or the sympathetic questions he put to me. It was the first time anyone had asked such questions or shown any genuine interest in what had really happened.

I told him that I knew now there was no way of going to school, no way of getting any sort of grant. I had to earn my living, and that was that. But it was no use trying to earn it in ways I was not cut out for. He was my last hope: if he couldn't help me, then I was going back to Germany.

'What? You – back to Germany?' He couldn't take it in. 'But you couldn't ever do that, could you?'

I explained that many of my friends were still there. They would give me more help than I'd ever get here.

'No,' he said. 'I won't hear of it.'

If I was so keen to take up radiography, he would do all he could for me. But he wanted to know how I had done in my examinations before I walked out. This was something I couldn't answer. I hadn't dared make enquiries, wasn't even sure I wanted to know, and in no circumstances was I going to go back, not even to work out my notice.

'He put his hand on my shoulder. 'All right, we'll see. I'll help you. Just leave it to me.' As he took his hand away he looked at the material of the green jacket I was wearing. 'Is that a uniform of some kind?'

I told him exactly what it was. It had been cut down from the coat of an S.S. woman I had helped to capture at the end of the war; and my hat had been made from the bits trimmed off the full-length coat. It still looked a bit like a uniform, but the buttons were different: originally they had carried the Nazi swastika, but the tailors in the workroom at the Displaced Persons camp had cut them off and substituted plain green buttons.

'You?' he marvelled. 'You, wearing an S.S. woman's coat?'

In a muddled way I tried to explain the psychological satisfaction it gave me. All the time when the rest of us were freezing, some freezing to death, we had envied the vicious bitches so snug in their waterproof, windproof coats. Now I had one for myself.

He did not look wary about me, doubting my sanity, as some might have done. 'One day,' he said gently, 'you must come over and tell me a lot more about it.' One day, I thought, perhaps I would write something about it. And he would be the first person to get a copy.

Having decided to adopt me, as it were, he spared no trouble. Right away he checked up on my examination results and found that in spite of the sister's gloomy predictions I had done very well. Then he went to London and discussed the matter with colleagues in the Faculty of Radiologists. Strictly speaking, matriculation level physics, chemistry and biology were required. But there was a loophole: students who had gone through basic nursing training were sometimes admitted, and it was decided to accept me on twelve months' probation. I was to live in at Birmingham's Royal Orthopaedic Hospital with board and lodging provided, and was paid as a probationer nurse. Dr Brailsford paid out of his own pocket for me to attend the necessary lectures. He was wonderful in so many ways. Then and later, without attracting the attention or jealousy of other staff or trainees, he would occasionally slip me an envelope with money in it, just to help me along.

Unfortunately I encountered another sister who took against a foreigner like me at once. 'Oh, somebody the doctor brought in,' she sneered about me in other people's presence. But this time I was not going to be beaten.

Accommodation was rather strange. While a new nurses' home was being built we had to share rooms in shops taken over by the hospital. Most student radiographers were installed above the original premises, but I had to share a shop window, painted over on the inside, with a girl who has since become a very good friend but who at first must have found me a deplorable room-mate. Our pasts were so different that for some time we could hardly communicate about anything. Margaret certainly would not have understood if in those days I had tried to tell her this wasn't the first time I had lived in a shop front, or to convey

the creepy feeling it gave me of being back in that far-off little community waiting for a 'requisition' or a 'marching order'.

In my spare time I went to the Birmingham International Centre,
where at least I had something in common with other European
refugees. Something, but not much: most of them had escaped before
the war and grown up in England; none had been in an extermination
camp; and in spite of the persecution which had driven them from
their homelands, none could quite grasp how much worse it had
become after their departure.

There was another refuge, this one for solitude rather than com-
panionship. At 7 a.m. we had to be on the wards, doing the beds and
bed-pans and so on. Then into the X-ray department for the rest of the
day except for the time spent at lectures. In the evening it was essential,
for me especially, to settle down to private study. This was not possible
with other girls chattering all round, so I used to shut myself away in
the city reference library until closing time; then I would often go on
to the International Centre, where a couple of boys helped me with
physics and chemistry.

The official timetable made no provision for such extramural work.
All trainees were supposed to be indoors by ten o'clock. I couldn't
bear to conform. I wasn't back in prison, was I? Or in a concentration
camp block with all the various curfews they imposed: *Blocksperre*,
Lagersperre, Lagerruhe . . .? 'Never obey.' It was a motto I had made up
for myself long ago.

By special permission we could get one late pass a week, but I stayed
out every single night, and after the Centre closed would take a long
walk back to my quarters. At one or two in the morning I often had to
climb in through other girls' rooms, up a drainpipe to whichever
window happened to be open. I never worried about how this might
disturb my fellow trainees or how Margaret would be upset when
word got round about her impossible room-mate. Scrambling into your
bunk in Auschwitz, you trampled over other girls as a matter of course.

Nor could I sympathize with Margaret's distress over my untidiness.
Beds in hospital had to be neat, and our own were supposed to be the
same. I rebelled against this and made a wilful shambles of my bed and,
indeed, the whole room. 'How can you live in such a mess?' poor
Margaret protested. 'I just can't stand it.' We were quite unsuited to
each other, yet somehow we made a go of it.

When my dragon of a sister got to hear rumours of my late hours,
she gleefully assured me I'd never get anywhere, spending half the
night out with a man. It never struck her that there might be other
reasons for staying out.

In fact, though, I did have a boy-friend, who was later to become my husband. Ralph had come to England at the age of thirteen with the very last transport of pre-war refugee children aboard the *Washington* in 1939. His seven-year-old brother was not accepted, and in due course went with their mother into the Auschwitz gas chambers. His father was imprisoned in Flossenbürg and was still alive in March 1945: he died just about a month before liberation. All other members of the family were wiped out save for one who reached South America. Ralph was quite alone. Like myself, he found the Jewish community less than helpful, but was looked after in a camp near Ipswich and then brought to Birmingham under the auspices of the Christadelphians. They were very kind to the children in their keeping, and never made the slightest attempt to sway any of them towards their own religious beliefs. At fifteen Ralph was sent out to earn his living, apprenticed to an upholstery firm. Many a time he walked back with me to the nurses' quarters and heaved me up over the fence. Oh, they were all so sure, the sister and my fellow probationers, that I was up to no good.

Ralph and I married in March 1949. Once more I was frowned on as a rebellious type. You were not supposed to marry during training. But we had found a leaky room and kitchenette at the top of a decrepit old Edgbaston house for £1 a week, and had to make a decision without delay. With the living-out allowance I'd be entitled to, we would just get by. I wrote urgently to Dr Brailsford, who was away on a lecture tour. Not so long before this he had made one girl leave the course because she insisted on marrying, but to the displeasure of the authorities he wrote me a charming letter, saying that of course I must get married, and wishing me every happiness.

We could afford only a spartan three-day honeymoon in Matlock. With exams imminent, most of that time had to be spent on last-minute revision, with Ralph questioning and prompting me. Everyone in the hospital was by now quite positive that I was too irresponsible ever to achieve anything.

In April I was the only girl in my year to qualify.

Dr Brailsford was delighted that I had not let him down, and gave me a dictionary as a commemorative present. Not only that: he at once offered me a full-time appointment in the Royal Orthopaedic Hospital, which meant regular, though small, earnings in addition to the living-out allowance I received.

Dr Brailsford was a wonderful man to work with. At Christmas he always presented his staff with books and for me he also had a special extra present which he passed to me discreetly, as with those envelopes of money. He was such an imposing figure, with such a high reputation in his profession, that I felt shy in his presence, and couldn't tell him how much his kindness meant to me. But I think he understood, and his generosity never slackened. And when he relaxed, he was great fun. On his sixtieth birthday he strode into the X-ray department and announced: 'Girls, we're shutting up shop. Right now. We're all going for a picnic.' Off we went in two cars to Malvern, and scampered about the hillside like children, with Dr Brailsford as boisterous as any of us.

As I began to feel more confident, a weird, nagging compulsion grew in me. Since the liberation I had done my best to like people and get on with them, even when some of them failed to understand this. I really longed to enjoy life and not be hostile and resentful. I kept telling myself there was no bitterness left in me, not any more. But all sorts of questions fidgeted on in my head.

At the International Centre I declared one day that if ever I had a little money to spare I would like to take a holiday in Germany.

'You, of all people!' All my friends were at once up in arms.

Still I felt I had to go back to Germany somehow, sometime, to find out what those people were really like in themselves, in their own country, in peacetime. In Auschwitz the Nazis had preached hatred and made sure it was hammered into everybody. The air was filled with it, forced on us by their calculated policy of wickedness. Like the lethal gas in the death chambers, once it had been released there was no way you could escape breathing it and dying from it. Official policy. German policy. In the end it made you distrust everybody: your fellow prisoners, prisoners of your own nationality, *everybody*. And in the outside world now, were things so different? Were the defeated Germans just shedding crocodile tears, biding their time until they could indulge their savagery again, the moment the opportunity presented itself?

It is impossible to go on being permanently hostile and cynical. Unrelenting hatred of the entire human race cannot be kept up forever; undying hatred of one nation surely cannot be right. Sooner or later I had to force myself to go to Germany and face these questions.

Strangely, I discovered quite early on that those who most vigorously denounce the Germans are those who never experienced anything really terrible themselves. The refugees who spent a comparatively comfortable war in England were and are much more rancorous than the death camp survivors.

My mother shared my feelings. She would never go back to Poland, to see our home town or our old home, and least of all to revisit

Auschwitz; but she, too, felt this compulsion to visit Germany. Only much later, when compensation for some of our losses began to come through, could either of us afford such a trip.

While working in the Children's Hospital I decided at last to have my concentration camp number cut out of my arm. This my mother would never contemplate. Only after her death in 1974 did I get permission to have her number also removed; and now it is in pickle along with my own. A gruesome relic; but such relics must be preserved. Some factions today deny that the holocaust ever took place. They claim that the whole thing is a conspiracy to defame that misjudged idealist, Hitler, and that nobody was ever gassed, nobody ever burnt in the crematoria. The passing years blur the facts, and by 1980 it was possible for there to be a French Nazi movement openly slandering and even murdering Jews, whose leader could declare in an interview:

'The stories about six million Jews being gassed by the Nazis are pure propaganda . . . No Jews were gassed in gas chambers. I reckon the gas chambers were built for propaganda purposes after the war.'

A few weeks later, a bomb attack on a Paris synagogue killed a large number and maimed many more.

As time goes on there are fewer and fewer of us left to testify that the abominations did happen; and when we are gone, there must be some evidence left so that nobody can hope to get away with denying the truth or twisting it to his own ends. The gas chambers were there. The murderers were there. Auschwitz was there, and its remains can still be seen, not 'built for propaganda purposes after the war'. I know, because I was there, waiting my turn which never came.

Four years after my mother's death I did what she wished me never to do: I went back to Auschwitz. Planning a series of programmes on women at war, Yorkshire Television approached me in 1978 to see if an episode could be built around my experiences. After some discussion they decided the story ought to be told at length rather than in one chapter of a series, and took me back to Poland for what turned out to be a film lasting an hour and three-quarters.

When the challenge came I was not at all sure I was up to it. You don't walk back into hell of your own free will. I appealed to one of my few fellow survivors to come with me and give me moral support. Henia was an attractive girl who had been spared the gas chambers because the commandant of the ghetto from which she was sent to Auschwitz could not bear to think of her being destroyed, and insisted on personally handing her and her family over to the camp commandant. I met her when she had contracted typhus and was brought to the hospital compound where I was working· and after evacuation of the camp we were on the long death march together. But she did not feel she could face going back.

So my companion would be my grown-up elder son, David. When he was little and always on the go, always keen to join in adult conversation, he had heard the name of Auschwitz only in veiled remarks and jokes between his grandmother and myself. Yes, jokes: not wanting to give the two boys frightening dreams, we had done our best to make only light-hearted passing references to the place. Some of the frugal habits my mother acquired in the camp could never be broken, and the boys would laugh about them: 'Oh, Granny's at it again – here, shove those bits and pieces in the fridge, mustn't throw this away, would never have done in Auschwitz . . .' Now David was old enough to come and see for himself.

The television company went to great trouble to get their facts right and help me in every way. First of all they visited my birthplace, Bielsko, a small south-western Polish town near the Czechoslovak border. The researchers hoped to find some remnant of my existence there, though all the odds seemed against it. But at the Notre Dame convent school I had attended as a girl they were incredibly lucky.

The Mother Superior, who in my days there had been a young nun, explained that towards the end of the war the Soviet Army had smashed through the place, torn out desks to make room for hospital wards in the building, and burnt most of the school records. When the place was eventually handed back to the Poles, they found just three folders of old class records: and one of them contained my first-year school report. In general, Kitty Felix's conduct appeared to have been 'satisfactory', and the prognosis for the future was 'promising'.

But Auschwitz, so few miles away, was what I really had to face. Even before leaving England I had begun to shiver, afraid I might never get home again. 'I can't escape a second time,' I said to myself. 'It can't be done, I'm sure it can't – not twice.'

The situation grew more incredible as we approached the gates. I had left the camp in November 1944, yet here it still was, waiting for me. The railway line still led up to the main gate and the ramp on to which hundreds of starving, stinking, half-dead men, women and children had been tipped from each incoming train, to be divided immediately into those who would go straight to the gas chambers and those who would be allowed to survive as slave labour for a few weeks or months. But this time I was not arriving by train in the middle of the night. It was a bright, cold, sunny day, and we were being driven up to the entrance in a white taxi. It was crazy.

Past and present got hopelessly jumbled up. All I could be sure of was that I belonged here. And anyway, there wasn't anywhere else in the world. Never had been, never would be. I was not visiting a deserted museum, years and years after some historic reality. No: I was seeing the camp as crowded as it had always been, hearing the crack of whips, the screams, the dogs, smelling the burning flesh.

It was insane, my being here again after so long. But no more so than the great insanity which had delivered me at these gates in the first place.

2

To the Ghetto

SOME FIFTEEN YEARS before first setting eyes on Auschwitz I opened my eyes on to a more attractive world in Bielsko, at the foot of the Beskidy mountains dividing Poland from Czechoslovakia. From my second birthday onwards my life was very active. I was taught swimming, skating and ski-ing, attended the local gymnastics club, took piano lessons, and gained a smattering of English in the nursery school where my mother was always encouraging the children to sing or recite English nursery rhymes and songs. Every weekend we went up into the hills.

The town was small but thriving, thanks largely to its textile industry, and was set in the most beautiful countryside. Shielded from winds by that mountain range, we had lovely hot summers and cold but dry and sunny winters. The view from my bedroom window was of a peak 3,000 feet high, and when the sun fell on it there was a glittering reflection from the windows of the tourist hut at the top. During the week I was impatient to be away, living only for the hours when I could be skating and ski-ing again.

My father was a lawyer by training but ultimately took over his father's agricultural supply business. He was away for long periods, at all hours of the day and evening, conducting most of his business in cafés and smoking incessantly. Since my mother was also preoccupied – with her teaching – a large part of my childhood was spent in the care of maids and nannies. Perhaps some hidden resentment about being left in such hands, together with envy of my elder brother Robert who always seemed to get whatever he asked for, made me something of a terror. When quite little I would sneak into classrooms where my mother was teaching, and hide under desks and pinch the girls' legs. I

ble to battle the canoe back up the river, I had simply carried it on to
train and travelled back in comfort.

Before our holiday was due to end we received a telegram from my
ther, telling us to pack and come home at once. My brother Robert,
venteen at the time and on holiday elsewhere with a group of friends,
as also summoned home. When we got to Bielsko we could hardly
elieve our eyes. All our furniture, clothes, linen, glass and carpets had
een crated up ready to be sent away. The rooms looked bare and
orlorn. People we knew were asking my father what he thought was
oing to happen, what they ought to do. Words like 'evacuation' and
nobilization' cropped up over and over again. At last my mother told
e there was almost certainly going to be a war. But I did not under-
tand who was going to fight whom, and what it had to do with us.

The answer was obvious enough in the streets of the town. The noise
ut there was far more menacing than the hollow echoes indoors.
Iooligans were smashing windows, and squads of Germans were
narching up and down waving flags bearing the Nazi swastika. All
retence was thrown aside. Because of Bielsko's position near both
zech and German borders, it had always had a mixed population. The
own had in fact belonged to different countries at various times. Three
anguages were in everyday use, and people got along together. Until
ow. Now there were machine-guns on the roofs of houses belonging
o German families, ready for the moment when they could start shoot-
ng down the Poles among whom they had lived for decades, some of
hem for generations.

Realizing how swiftly the storm was mounting, my father had
ecided it was high time for us to get out. He had an idea that things
vould be better in central Poland, further away from the so frequently
ontested frontier, and picked on Lublin. It was slightly to the east of
entre, actually; but the Russians were thought to be less of a threat than
he Germans.

Our furniture and household goods were sent off by train and on
4 August we followed, taking my maternal grandmother with us. We
vere lucky to get seats on one of the few passenger trains which had
not been cancelled. Many refugees had to walk, loaded down with
heir belongings on their backs. We travelled in reasonable comfort,
vith a small suitcase each.

Lublin is one of Poland's most historic cities, with an impressive
ixteenth-century cathedral and some very fine old buildings. But I
nated it. I wanted to go home. It was impossible to believe that I would
not soon be back training in the swimming pool, working in the
gymnasium, spending weekends in the mountains again.

was forever climbing trees, and was once trapped in on<
rescued; I got my fingers caught in a mangle, playing
shouldn't have been; and I often stirred up violent quar
girls and attacked them.

Nannies never lasted long in our household. The)
controlling me indoors. And if we went out for a walk,
of hiding until they went home without me. I liked go
schools, especially in winter when we were allowed ski-
but even then I could not restrain my tomboyish unrulin
end of the first week my parents were accustomed to rec
pleas from the organizers for my instant removal.

At last it was decided to send me into the stricter dis
local convent school. This was the best school in town,
run by Catholic nuns had a large proportion of Jewish gii
excused the religious sessions. Even here I didn't quiet<
picked quarrels with other girls, and automatically did th<
whatever the nuns wished me to do. 'Who says so?' mig
my motto. This sounds unruly and aggressive, but it wa
which was to stand me in good stead. It was not so much
defiance of all authority as a questioning of where that aut
from. 'Never obey' – not mechanically, unquestioningly, tl
the real troubles came, outward defiance was fatal; but I
this inner refusal to surrender or to believe a word that
me – least of all words that were shouted or screamed at me
came I was already mentally alert, and physically tough fror
gymnastics.

In 1939 I won a bronze medal swimming for Poland agains
As the youngest member of the team, I was proud of my ac
At the same time I was disturbed by the way Jewish meml
team were jeered at by our fellow Poles. This was my first
with anti-Semitism, and it made no sense. I had to put it
mind as I prepared for the next round, and also went into tra
the gymnastic and junior athletic teams. I was not at all glad t
away by my parents for our usual mountain holiday, this tin
the High Tatra in southern Poland. Once we were there,
loved every minute of it: the last holiday of its kind I was to
long, long time. Of course I had to cause trouble, as usual.
after my father had gone back to Bielsko and his business ther
my mother and myself to carry on enjoying ourselves, I too
out on the treacherous river Dunajec and was away for hou\
parties had been sent out to look for me by the time I got b
return trip was a bit different from the outgoing one: as it wa

At dawn on 1 September 1939, Hitler's troops invaded Poland, while his air force bombed military and civilian targets indiscriminately. As their advance continued and Polish defenders retreated, bombs showered down on Lublin. The house next door to the one in which we were lodging was set ablaze, and all our windows were blown out.

My father had been plodding to and from the city's railway stations in search of our belongings, which ought to have arrived well before we did. There was no sign of them. At last we learned they had been lost in a train which was bombed and destroyed in Cracow station.

Within a matter of weeks German troops came marching into Lublin to find deserted streets, bolted doors, and barricaded windows. My first reaction was one of childish admiration. Peeping out through the shutters or from a doorway, I thought the soldiers looked so brave and held themselves so splendidly. When I ventured out into the streets, as we all did sooner or later, if only out of curiosity, the men were even more impressive: they had such fantastic uniforms and black boots, and I remember them parading across the city with a baton waving and a band playing.

The fact that they were out to crush people like me was soon made clear. One important decree was that when German soldiers walked along a pavement, everyone else had to step off into the gutter. The first time such a situation arose in my case, I didn't do this but simply turned my head away. At once the man set about me, and I arrived home limping and badly bruised. But I was lucky to get away so lightly. Shortly afterwards, I was walking along with the son of an acquaintance of my father's, when a couple of Germans appeared on the pavement ahead. I stepped off; the boy didn't. One of the Germans immediately pulled out his gun and shot my friend through the head, killing him instantly. We were getting a glimmering of what was in store for all of us.

Very soon posters went up ordering all Jews to declare themselves. No Jew was allowed out of doors without an armband bearing the Star of David. Even with an armband you were by no means safe: any German could suddenly seize you and drag you off to shovel snow or polish Nazi boots, and to add to the humiliation it was quite common for girls to have their heads shaved before they were allowed to go back to their families. Laws were enacted forbidding Jewish children to attend any school whatsoever, and no Jew was allowed to continue his trade or profession.

My brother, like many of the men, decided to flee. He hoped to join up with some Polish partisan force still resisting the Germans, or maybe get right away and somehow reach our aunt and uncle in

England and then join the British Army. My father could not bring himself to leave my mother, grandmother, and myself.

Although no Jew was allowed to practise medicine, and getting hold of equipment and materials was difficult anyway, some struggled to help their fellows. One of these was a dentist who set up a makeshift surgery in his bedroom. My father, afraid that with too much time on my hands I might get into mischief, suggested I might act as the dentist's receptionist and assistant. One of my most important duties was to keep a lookout for inquisitive Germans and help hide equipment under the bed or in the pantry. While I was employed in this way, and enjoying it, my father also arranged for some of my back teeth to be filled with small diamonds which he had managed to bring in his hand luggage. 'You may need them one day,' he said. He could scarcely have foreseen just how much I would need them or in what circumstances.

Soon even our limited freedom was taken from us. All Jews were rounded up and herded into the eastern end of the city, where the Germans were creating an enclosed ghetto. Now they knew exactly where we were and could deal with us in earnest.

The S.S., Hitler's personally created *Schutzstaffel* or Defence Corps, whose *Einsatzgruppen* or Special Action Groups knew more about assaulting individuals than defending them, began to produce a whole series of ransom demands. The Jewish Council would be peremptorily ordered to produce 1,000 wedding rings by the next day. When the next day came there might be a further demand for 100 chairs or 100 sheets or blankets. If these were not forthcoming, batches of inhabitants would be deported. Nobody knew their destination. 'Resettlement' was the word: a deceptive, meaningless word. In addition, every now and then a party of S.S. would go on a destructive rampage, not collecting booty but simply smashing up everything in their path. As a result of all these demands and savage raids, there was soon barely a stick of furniture left in the ghetto, and the drain on valuables meant there was little left with which to buy food.

Such food as the inhabitants of the ghetto were officially allowed was obtained only by ration cards. The allowance was just above starvation level. New repressive laws prohibited milk, eggs and meat in Jewish households. Not that we had much chance of getting hold of such food. If any was found during a German raid it would be thrown away, and the family might be taken off and never seen again. Cooking of any kind was forbidden. Nobody was allowed out of the ghetto to work or barter for extra rations, nor were we allowed to have money, other than an internal currency, valueless outside and not much use inside.

If in spite of everything you had managed to hang on to a few valuables, then it was possible to do a deal with the Poles on the other side of the barbed wire. Possible, but dangerous: you had to crawl out on to forbidden territory and take the risk of having whatever you offered grabbed and then being betrayed. The Lublin Poles were utterly corrupt. They waited eagerly for Jews to come out so they could profit from the misery of those who until a few months before had been their fellow citizens.

Foraging was often done by children, since the risk was greater for adults. I regularly took off my compulsory yellow star and went over to the 'Aryan' side with coins and trinkets given to me from my father's dwindling resources, exchanging little things we had treasured for a few crusts of bread or slices of salami. It was not easy. My accent was not a local one, and Poles would guess I was Jewish. I was caught and beaten black and blue more than once. If reported to the Nazis, an adult risked being executed on the spot, or after a sadistic parody of an interrogation. On one occasion, with a couple of hard-won loaves under my arm, I was pounced on by a German N.C.O. and hustled off to scrub the floors of the officers' quarters in neighbouring barracks. When I had finished, he stamped over everything I had done, screaming abuse.

'What's this? Call that floor clean?' He hit me about the head. 'I'll show you how to clean a floor. Come on, get down to it.' And I had to do it all over again before I was thrown out and allowed to scuttle back into the ghetto – without my bread.

A compulsive smoker, my father longed for cigarettes almost as much as for bread and meat. I managed during a few sorties to get some tobacco leaves, and these were hung on a line in our room to dry. We chopped up the leaves and he rolled them like a cigar in any sort of paper he could find: there was no cigarette paper. It meant so much to him that I was curious to try it for myself. Rolling up leaves in the same way, I started to smoke.

The raids went on. Looting and bullying and unpredictable arrests continued. Neighbours co-operated in an attempt to fool the tormentors. Many houses were joined together by tunnels between their cellars, and warnings could be hurried through from one building to the next all along a street. Signals would be passed from one side of the street to the other, a white rag waved in a window or a swift sign with the fingers to announce that a raiding party was on its way. Cupboards were converted into hiding-places. Secret openings were made in walls and behind fireplaces. But the calculated persecution could only be slowed or dodged for a brief while. It could not be brought to a standstill.

One question above all is repeatedly put to survivors of the Holocaust. Why, when the number of Jews threatened was so enormous, was there so little open resistance? Even in the face of bayonets and machine-guns wouldn't it have been worth attempting a concerted rush at the enemy?

People who ask this can have no idea of the circumstances prevailing at the time. In the first place, nobody in his wildest fantasies guessed the extent of the massacre which the Nazis had in mind. If today a Jewish, Jamaican, Chinese, Muslim or Jehovah's Witness community in Liverpool, Wolverhampton or London was warned that its members were to be rounded up and put in preventive detention, would any of them believe or guess that they were destined to be converted into fertilizer and ersatz soap? Even towards the end of the Second World War, in spite of detailed reports, photographs and incontrovertible evidence smuggled out to the Allies, a large number of well-informed people still refused to believe in the existence of this remorseless genocide; and, to their shame, a number of those who knew it must be true still did not want the facts publicized or have anything done about the problem.

For those of us on the spot, there was a confusion which the Germans deliberately encouraged. In Lublin, most local Jews were swiftly deported from the ghetto to make way for dazed newcomers, so that few remained who really knew their way about the district. As the war spread, Jews who had been brought in on transports from Holland, France and elsewhere were dumped in the ghetto and left to find their own feet. Such few Polish Jews as had managed to remain found difficulty communicating through language barriers.

All money brought in was invalid. Newcomers received no immediate issue of local currency with which to buy food, so in exchange for bread they had to part with what valuables they still possessed. Even as they struggled to get their bearings they were shipped out so that another batch could be moved in. There was no time to co-ordinate any mass movement against the oppressors. Lublin, like several other ghettoes, was basically a giant transit camp with a constantly shifting population. Moreover, effective resistance would have required help from non-Jewish Poles in the rest of the city. This was rarely forthcoming. You paid dearly for every contribution from outside. Throughout history there has often been strongly anti-Semitic feeling in Poland among certain elements, and now they not only allowed the Germans to do what they liked with Polish Jews but actively collaborated with the invader. A few showed genuine compassion and courage, but others were only too glad to find Jews in hiding and hand them over to the Nazis.

It must also be understood that the Lublin Poles were largely uneducated and had little grasp of the over-all picture. It was a different matter in Warsaw when the ghetto held out for four weeks in 1943 against the S.S. There the better-educated and sympathetic townsfolk offered invaluable assistance. The commandant in his report sounds genuinely reproachful that 'the Jews no longer had any intention to resettle voluntarily, but were determined to resist evacuation'. *Resettle* . . .! The Warsaw example served as an inspiration for later uprisings in Lvov, Vilna, and other places – even, in due course, in Lublin.

In our time the inhabitants of the Lublin ghetto did not really grasp what the continuing outflow meant. We were told that those who departed were on their way to labour camps and would be building fortifications. The Germans were extending their defences all over conquered Europe, and it made grim sense that transports should be carrying Jews for slave labour on such projects. The full truth – that extermination was to take priority over any work the captives might be capable of – was too fantastic for most people to believe until they were actually in the gas chamber and beginning to inhale the poison. Nevertheless a few, alarmed or angered by being treated like cattle, did strike back, turning on their oppressors and fighting with their bare hands. It was as swift a way as any of committing suicide.

The best resistance was not to pit oneself against the heavily armed S.S., but to escape, to join the partisans said to be operating away in the south, in Romania . . . anywhere.

After their pact with Hitler the Russians had moved into Poland from the east in 1939 as far as the river Bug. Until almost the end of 1940 this frontier remained open, and refugees from the German occupation crossed regularly into the Russian zone. In that winter of late 1940 my father decided we must head in that direction. He hired a peasant with a horse and cart to take us east. Looking back, I can't imagine where he found the man or how he paid him. Did my mother or grandmother give up some pieces of jewellery? Or did I? It's a complete blank in my mind.

But I remember the horse and cart well enough. Dressed as peasants, we huddled on the cart through bitter rain and sleet. It was a dreadful journey. Sometimes the mud and slush were so deep that the wheels sank in, and the horse could not pull them out. We had to get down and push the cart free, often up to our knees in freezing cold mud. And then there was snow.

It was illegal to travel by night, but even more dangerous to do so by day as far as we were concerned. We covered as much ground as possible during the hours of darkness, and during the day hid the cart in the woods. We were cold and wretched, but perhaps those awful conditions were a blessing in one way: there were few other people on the roads, and the Germans did not venture out in that weather if they could help it, least of all at night. It was amazing that my grandmother survived the journey: she was almost seventy and a diabetic. She stayed on the cart even when the rest of us had to push it out of the mire, and we kept her wrapped in as many coats and blankets as we could muster.

One night, close to exhaustion, we risked staying in a small village. We were very reluctant to move on again, but my father insisted that we must not linger. It was a good thing he was so insistent. We were only a few miles away when the Germans descended on the place for a round-up.

Our destination was Dorohusk, a village on the river Bug. When at last we reached it, we found it crammed with refugees like ourselves. We could not understand why so many were waiting on this side of the river. Then we were told that the frontier had been closed twenty-four hours earlier. Our journey had been fatally slowed by bad roads and weather. Among the refugees were, to our amazement, my father's cousin Max with his wife Lucy, and a remarkable amount of luggage. They helped us find a room in a cottage which we shared with about twenty other people.

Those who had got this far were in no mood to turn back. Nearly all of them, like us, were determined to cross the river somehow. Unfortunately it was a very wide river, with Germans patrolling this side of it and Russian sentries now on the alert on the other bank. But if you *could* reach that far side undetected and walk the many miles to the nearest sizeable town, it ought not to be too difficult to disappear into the crowd. The Russians were not systematically looking for Jews, and even if you fell into their hands, you might get away with being sent to Siberia to work.

Rowing across was too slow and too risky. Some who attempted it were shot. The best plan was to wait for the river to freeze and then race across it by sleigh.

The waiting was interminable. There was only one thing to be thankful for: although large numbers of troops were stationed nearby to guard the frontier, the local villages were too scattered and insignificant to attract the attentions of the Gestapo or the S.S. – so far, anyway. Until the river froze, we had to find money to pay for food and our cramped accommodation. Father applied for a job in a nearby sawmill. It was in German hands, but the superintendent was so glad to have someone fluent in both Polish and German that he asked no questions.

Weeks dragged on. Still the river refused to ice over. Several of us set about learning Russian. My father and others sounded out local guides who would know the best way across when the time came. We took it in turns to keep watch on patrols along both banks, noting the times they changed when a dash might be made.

During the past fifteen months I had learned a lot and no longer asked childish questions. There was no going back to my schooldays, the swimming pool or the ski-ing in the beautiful mountains. Now I was teaching myself to be always alert, suspicious of every sound and shadow, always ready to run, or hide, or crouch absolutely still. I studied the patrols and memorized their timetables and movements. When someone tried to cross at night and there were shots and yells and then silence I had learned not to flinch – and tried not to imagine what it would be like if, when we made a break for it, we were fired on.

At last the river froze.

My father's cousin Max and his wife were among the first to risk the crossing. They were horrified when the driver of the sleigh told them he had no intention of loading up all their luggage. He wanted to move fast, and he wasn't going to carry all that stuff across the ice. This was no time for luxuries. So off they went, leaving all their belongings behind. But they did at any rate get through safely.

Then it was our turn. Conditions seemed just right. The driver of the sleigh was ready for us and thought we could be across in a few minutes by a route he had checked and rechecked. The night was pitch black, and there was just enough wind to cover any sounds we might make, unless we were very unlucky. We helped my grandmother aboard, and packed ourselves in around her. The driver raced his horse and sleigh out on to the ice, and we were away. I held my breath. Now the Germans would start shooting. They must surely see us on that white expanse, which seemed to have an eerie light of its own.

'We're nearly there,' my father whispered.

Nearly there. Come on, only a few more yards. We reached the other bank, and still no Germans had spotted us. We'd made it; we were safe.

Suddenly there was a volley of shots. Bullets howled overhead. We threw ourselves down in the sleigh. Spurts of snow were kicked up by another burst of firing. The Russians were shooting at us. Before we could decide whether to scramble out and run for it, or roll under cover of the bank and hope the sentries would be distracted by something else, the driver made up his mind. He had no intention of hanging around as a target for the Russians. Without hesitation he swung the sleigh round and raced us back to the German side of the river. A few stray bullets screeched along the ice after us, but we got back unscathed: back where we had started.

The sleigh driver was anxious to make himself scarce before the Germans began to investigate the commotion. He went his way, we rushed back to our room. We hadn't been there long before a patrol burst in, looking for those who had made a bid to cross the frontier. When they demanded to see our identity papers, they were taken aback by our fluent German. On top of that, my father produced a certificate stating that he had served as an officer in the Austrian Army, and then dug out a row of medals to confirm this. The N.C.O. in charge jerked his squad to attention, and saluted. 'Heil Hitler!' Confronted by my father's insistence that we were Germans stranded by the awful weather on our way to our home town in the Fatherland, he apologized for the intrusion and left, with a promise to report the matter and see that we were helped on our way.

It was a promise we would have been happy to do without. Once our respectful friend got back to base and reported the existence of this ex-Austrian officer with medals and a travel problem, someone was bound to come and investigate. We had to move, and move fast. Already there was talk of the Germans evacuating the civilian population from the border region. Either we made one more dash for it, or we turned back.

'We can't go back to Lublin, not after everything that's happened.' That was one thing we said, one after the other, over and over again. And then: 'We daren't risk another crossing. It won't work.'

Any minute now the helpful Germans would come looking for us, and cease being friendly once they discovered who we really were. It had to be Lublin. We hated the place, but at least we still had some friends there, and it was better to be among friends than wandering helplessly about the countryside from one group of strangers to another. We gathered up the possessions which Cousin Max and Lucy had left behind. Max wouldn't be back for them. The beautiful clothes, silk stockings and other luxuries would be useful to tide us over, bartered for food.

After another bleak, wintry journey we were back in the ghetto.

3

On the Run

CONDITIONS IN Lublin had worsened during our absence. Very little furniture remained in any of the houses, and the food situation was desperate. S.S. raids took place almost nightly. So it was back to the trips into the city, to scheme and barter for bread. We were glad of Cousin Lucy's expensive wardrobe.

In spite of the risks, my mother now began to venture across the barrier. She did more than her share in winning food for us by teaching English to carefully chosen and recommended adult pupils.

Who on earth, though, would want to learn English at a time like this? Perhaps for some it was a way of filling in the time; or a mute gesture of defiance, allying themselves in spirit with the British who were at war with Germany and must therefore be Poland's friends; it would enable people to listen secretly to B.B.C. news bulletins and understand what was being said; and perhaps some hoped that one fine day they would be able to greet the liberators in their own language. It was probably a mixture of all these motives. Anyway, we had cause to be grateful for the supplementary rations this thirst for knowledge brought.

One of my mother's favourite pupils was a Roman Catholic priest, Father Krasowski, whose vicarage was right opposite Gestapo head-quarters. Having taken off her armband, my mother would walk out to visit him three times a week. He was deeply concerned about our welfare and insisted that if ever we needed his help and he was capable of giving it, we must not hesitate to get in touch.

One night a full-scale assault was launched on the ghetto. Without warning the whole area was encircled by troops with tanks and machine-guns. Then the round-up parties stormed in. They burst into houses and dragged the occupants out into the street, breaking up families and clubbing down anyone who tried to protest. Groups of dazed men, women and children were kicked into some sort of formation and marched off. This time there were no glib assurances of 'resettlement': those who left had gone for good, and we would never see them again.

Three such round-ups took place within a very short time. During the first we were among the victims driven out into the street. Once again my father did his party piece. Flourishing the document stating he had served as an officer in the Austrian Army, he grew so indignant with a German soldier that the men led us to shelter in the doorway of a house already emptied.

When the second raid came, we'd had enough advance warning to cram into a hiding-place within the house. On the third occasion we got off the street only minutes before lorries drove in and children were tossed from windows, men and women thrown bodily downstairs. A boy I had known in Bielsko was with me, and there was not room for all of us in the hiding-place. Hans and I wriggled under a bed. As jackboots stamped in and out of the echoing rooms, I began to shudder and wanted to cry. Hans put his arms around me; held me tight; heard a whimper starting in my throat and clamped his hand over my mouth. We clung together as boots thudded closer – then went away.

It was obvious that the Germans intended to clear the whole place, presumably to make room for a host of newcomers. For weeks we scurried from one refuge to another, hiding in cellars and sewers. It couldn't go on like this. Sooner or later they would catch up with us. Father decided we must have another try at getting out before we were carted out. But which direction to take? There was every reason to believe that the most brutal and dangerous conditions were in Poland. We must leave our country altogether. No question of going west or north-west, which would take us into Germany itself. Due north, we would be in Poland all the way until we reached the Russian-held lands along the Baltic, which offered us no hope. We had tried the east and been forced back. Now it had to be the south. If we could get through Czechoslovakia, Hungary and Yugoslavia to a port in Turkey, or even in Palestine, there might be some faint chance of getting away to England. It was a wildly remote chance, but there was no alternative.

We made up bundles of a few bedclothes with one change of clothes and underclothes, each wrapped in a sheet. My mother, grandmother and I would carry these on our backs. We could not make the bundles too heavy, not knowing how far we would have to walk. The strict curfew made it too dangerous to leave the ghetto at night. Whatever risks daylight might offer, we had to wait for the dawn. Then, removing our Jewish armbands, we simply walked out and hoped no German patrol would notice us, or that no sly collaborator would report us. If anyone had insisted on checking our papers, our journey would have come to an abrupt end.

This lack of documents was a constant danger. Every traveller had to register in every municipality where he intended to stay more than two days, and had to produce an *Abmeldeschein*, or exit permit. Since Jews were forbidden to travel at all, they could never possess this certificate. Our only chance was to find a Jewish community, and then make our way to another, and so on to others – if there were any left.

We struck out across country. I was not sure my father knew where he was taking us, but he led us on through forests and across fields, keeping well away from the roads. On a road we would have been too conspicuous. A patrol would inevitably have stopped us and asked for papers. Again we tried to travel mainly by night, this time without a horse and cart.

It was now that I began to understand how much like an animal a human being is. You *have* to be, in time of stress. Basic animal requirements are food, sleep, and the ability to excrete. Everything else is a bonus. Nobody who has not been on the run across hostile countryside, then driven to exhaustion as a slave labourer, then bullied and driven closer to death in an extermination camp, hungry for months on end – so hungry that most of the time it is impossible to think of anything else – can know how trivial everything else is. Permitted those three, you can survive: food ... sleep ... shit.

We had no map. My father did not dare to approach anyone to ask the way. Fortunately it was early summer and there was food in the woods and copses. We slept at the very edge of forests, not going in too deep in case we were taken unawares by patrolling dogs. A couple of times I ventured into peasant farmhouses to barter for food, and we hurried away afterwards before the farmer could have second thoughts about us. We must have followed a roundabout route, for the village we reached at last was not much more than fifteen miles from Lublin. Here in Zabia Wola there remained a small Jewish farming community of about fifteen families, swollen somewhat by refugees from towns in the region. Father decided we must stay here a while and recuperate after the tensions of the ghetto, Dorohusk, and now this latest journey. The only accommodation he could find was behind a little shop front. This was the first but not the last time I had to sleep virtually in a shop window.

Money was needed for food and to pay the rent. There was no employment in the village itself. No one wanted to give my father work in the fields, and it would be dangerous to travel anywhere else in search of a temporary job. Once again my mother came to the rescue. The little community was surrounded by large estates owned by the Polish aristocracy, many of them sheltering fellow noblemen who had been dispossessed by the Russians in eastern Poland and had fled west across the river Bug. The nearest landowner, Count Breza, welcomed my mother with open arms when she approached him with the suggestion that she should teach English in return for food. He introduced her to a number of his friends, and soon she was giving lessons on three different estates to the noblemen and their guests, intelligent and well-educated men who needed some such interest to keep them occupied. It meant a lot of walking for her, with the danger of being stopped and questioned by a German patrol. But she had a remarkable run of luck.

My father, too, was taken on by Count Breza, who was glad to have his library properly reorganized and catalogued. As for myself, I taught some of the smaller children reading, writing and arithmetic, and worked on the estate planting and harvesting sugar beet. In return we were given bread, or flour to make our own, and farm produce.

Our stay in Zabia Wola lasted longer than we had anticipated. A year went by, and we were feeling settled, healthy and at ease. My father was able to smoke a lot more now, rolling his own cigar-cigarette mixture from leaves I gathered for him. I even had a boy-friend, my very first. His name was Simon, and he was the son of the woman in whose shop we lodged. To be honest he was extremely ugly, almost freakish with a sort of twisted, frog-like face, but so good-natured that it didn't matter. I grew fonder and fonder of him. We both had mouth-organs and used to play a lot of music, and every now and then we danced with others of our own age. I knew nothing about sex. Even when we were together, just the two of us, in the shop front – which happened rarely – I didn't understand the occasional odd sensations he aroused in me. There was nothing physical between us, yet we were very close.

It was too good to last. We were doing nobody any harm, certainly not the Germans, and we could all have worked on contentedly enough until the end of the war. But word of this little Jewish society's existence had somehow leaked out and been passed on to a Nazi official. Along came the inevitable squads with the inevitable requisitions. For a while we didn't feel the full impact because father, mother and myself were away from the village most days. But every few days there would be a fresh demand: ten dozen eggs had to be handed over within six hours, or maybe it would be ten pairs of leather boots, or a dozen watches. The elders of the community scurried about making sure the demands were met. Otherwise there would be a *Marschbefehl* or marching order, meaning transportation to an unknown destination. We had known it before, and here it was again, the same old story.

Father heard disturbing news from Count Breza. He and his friends had more contact with the outside world, and what they reported convinced my father and mother that it was time to move on again. Soon there was bound to be an impossible demand, and then a round-up, and we would be finished. The village elders kept trying to appease the Germans, but the Germans didn't want to be appeased: they just wanted to play their dirty game until there was nothing left to play for.

One day there was panic. A large sum of money had to be handed over within twenty-four hours. There was no way of producing it, and the Germans knew it; even if by some miracle we had been able to raise the amount it would not have satisfied their appetite. A few days later there would have been another imposition and eventually, whatever we did, a round-up. When we admitted that the money could not be found, all the inhabitants of the village were served with a marching order for the following day. The Germans implied that the whole place was to be emptied and all Jews sent to a ghetto. Later, much later, we were to learn that this was not true. They were all in fact sent direct to Belzec camp and liquidated. At the time the full scale of the murder programme was something even we, from Lublin, had not begun to grasp; nor did we then have any idea that Zabia Wola was almost in the centre of a ring of extermination camps.

That night nobody undressed and nobody slept. At least we had been given warning. It was a time for decisions. Off and on, as German pressure increased, some of the younger people had talked about running into the forest and trying to locate a group of partisans. Simon talked just the way my brother Robert had talked. We were young, but we could fight. We didn't know where the partisans were, but we could find them. It was a tempting thought. Polish forests are deep and dense and wonderful, stretching for miles. The usual word for them, *puszcza*, implies a virtual jungle. We knew of wild boar still roaming there and often heard packs of wolves howling. Simon and his friends urged me to join them while there was still time – join them and hit back. At the same time my father was saying that the family must move on, must keep moving south.

I wanted to go with Simon. All night my father talked to me, and I kept insisting I wanted to fight instead of run.

'Do you imagine the partisans will want anyone as young as you?'
he asked. And then: 'If we part now, you know, we may never see
each other again.'

It was cruel. I was sure I ought to set off with the others, but felt
that both my father and mother needed my support. And there was my
grandmother as well.

'You've got to make up your own mind,' my father said at last. 'It's
up to you, my dear. I won't say another word.'

Before dawn came I said goodbye to Simon. There was an awful
sick emptiness inside me as he and a handful of our friends slipped
away from the village. I was sure I had made the wrong decision. And
as it turned out there wasn't my grandmother to be looked after. She
had had enough of running. Also, if we were to stand any chance of
escape, it would be better not to have her with us. While Simon and I
had been having our last talk, my mother and father must have been
arguing with my grandmother. I don't know who settled it in the end,
whether my grandmother said we must leave her because she wasn't
going to budge another inch, or whether my parents had to make up
their own minds and decide to leave her behind. But leave her we did.

We crept out before first light. From odd noises here and there we
gathered that the Germans were already moving into position, covering
the village with machine-guns. But it was August and the corn was
high, and we crawled unseen on all fours until we reached the nearest
woods. As the sun came up we reached a clearing from which the
village could be seen with the morning glow on its roofs, looking
snug and comfortable.

Suddenly there was a burst of machine-gun fire. A signal, maybe; or
just to frighten everyone. Then there were screams. The Germans
were rushing in and beating up our friends who had stayed behind.
After a while there was silence.

We could not dawdle. On we went through the woods. For about
three weeks we lived in the forest on little else but berries. We had
brought some scraps of food with us, but they didn't last long. We
had to ration ourselves, and it would not be long before there were no
rations and no berries. In the end my mother went to one of the
houses where she had taught English. The nearest to our escape route
was the estate of Baron Turnau, who was none too pleased to see her.
He knew what was going on and wanted no part of it. But his admiration for my mother outweighed his sense of the personal risks he was
running, and he promised to send one of his foresters to meet us if we
could all three reach the borders of his land undetected. Then we
might take shelter for a while in his hunting lodge.

My mother came back to collect us. We were in a ragged state and obviously on the run. Anyone who saw us out in the open would report us at once. Nevertheless we had to chance it. Dazed by the sunlight, we crept out of hiding and dodged from one patch of wooded cover to the next. To make things worse, I began to feel sick and dizzy. I could hardly walk. My father supported me part of the way, and then I think he had to carry me. I remember very little about it other than that dreadful feverish feeling. What happened after we reached the edge of the estate is like a blurred nightmare. I know the forester was there, waiting for us. He led us along narrow tracks through soaring trees to the hunting lodge. He wasn't happy about it. The Germans had been there once already with dogs, maybe hoping to track down some of the young people who had fled from Zabia Wola; if they came back, there was no telling what would happen.

I lay on a heap of straw in the loft. It was so good to rest. I didn't really care what happened next. That night or the night after, I am not sure which, I heard dogs barking and yelping. In my feverish state I thought they were scrambling up the walls outside and then clawing and snarling all over me. But I couldn't move. Instead of being a help to my parents, I was a burden.

The forester let the searchers in on the lower floor, assuring them there was nobody here. After a lot of thumping and snuffling about they went away. The forester was sure they would try again. The dogs would lead the way back to the lodge, and if they persisted and went through the building from top to bottom it would be all up with us – and with the forester and his master. As soon as daylight came he led us back to the edge of the forest where he proposed to leave us. Father protested that I was sick. After a lot of argument the man left us and went up to the big house. I was feeling worse than ever, and couldn't tell how long he was away. When he came back it was to say that Baron Turnau would take my mother and me in. But it was too risky to have my father on the premises. Father made up his mind on the spot. We must rest and I must get well, while he risked going by train to Lublin, of all places. He'd had an idea. We must trust him, and he would get in touch as soon as he could.

Mother and I were taken into the house and I was put to bed. The baron sent for a doctor, who at once diagnosed jaundice. He visited regularly and put me on a special diet, which I seem to remember was based largely on rice. Baron Turnau did not want any of the refugees of his own class to know we were there, so my mother and I were shut away in one room. He told us we could stay until I was well enough to move, but then we must go. Ironical, when you think of it: I was to be nursed back to health and then turned loose to get killed.

Just as I was getting better we had a message from my father. He told us where he was hiding in Lublin, and asked us to come at once. Mother thanked Baron Turnau, who was obviously upset by the thought of what might lie ahead of us. Then, without documents, we walked a long way to the nearest station and boarded a train for Lublin.

My father was hiding in the coal-shed of Father Krasowski's vicarage, across the street from Gestapo H.Q. The priest had been as good as his word. Asked for help, he gave it. Mother was delighted to see him again. I thought he was wonderful, so big and hearty and full of life, with such a blotchy red face from his heavy drinking that we nick-named him Father Tomato.

With the few remaining diamonds my father had managed to save, the priest had obtained false passports and papers for the three of us. Birth certificates, identity cards, everything. Before we could move on, we had to spend a few days in the coal-shed familiarizing ourselves with our new identities.

From now on my name was to be Leokadia Dobrzynska. My mother was to become my aunt. Father was apparently no relation to us at all. And now he broke the news to us. He was not going to travel with us. Both he and the priest explained earnestly that we would have a much better chance if we split up. After heart-rending arguments we had to agree.

The plan devised by the two men for my mother and myself was outrageous. They wanted us to go and work in Germany.

'You must understand,' Father Krasowski urged, 'the Germans are still busy rounding up Polish Jews. They know there are many of them with forged documents, just like yours.'

'But in Germany,' said my father, 'all Jews have been captured by now, and sent to various camps long ago. They do not expect to find Jews in Germany. So you will be safer there than here.'

It made sense, but what crazy sense! How monstrous, that we should be expected to contribute to the Nazi war effort! Nevertheless, that was our only hope of survival. If we attached ourselves to one of the batches of non-Jewish Poles being sent to the Reich for factory work, we might well pass unnoticed. My father gave me last-minute instructions. Although my birth certificate gave Lublin as my birth-place I had to remember to say, if asked, that I had not actually lived there for a long time but had just been visiting. In whatever group we joined, the other Poles would be local and might soon detect I was not one of them. Certainly I didn't have the local accent.

When the moment came, we had no time for lengthy farewells. Father Krasowski arrived, breathless, to say that a round-up of Polish labour had been made in his own church, during service. Kochmalna Street, near one of the railway stations, was the assembly point. People were being driven into it and kept there behind road blocks and armed guards. Some were fighting to get out. In the commotion my mother and I had no difficulty slipping into the street. Nobody was guarding against that.

Men and women were separated and driven into different parts of a waiting train. Or maybe there was more than one train: maybe one for the men, one for the women. In the confusion it was impossible to tell. Husbands and wives screamed and fought as they were dragged apart. Mother and I stayed close together and let ourselves be carried along on the tide. Now we were in the train, a passenger train, packed in with other women sobbing and shouting and arguing. Everyone wanted to tell everyone else where she had been picked up and caught for the labour market. Some were from the church, some had been simply swept up off the street.

Mother and I sat as still as we could, not daring to speak to each other. If we gave any inkling that we were Jewish, some of the others, even though they too were captives of the Nazis, might try to win favour by handing us over.

The train began to draw out of the station. We were on our way west, into the Reich.

4

The Dancing Lesson

WE TRAVELLED for two days. The journey was slow and not very comfortable, but I was glad to rest and have the chance of catching up on all my lost sleep. Mother drowsed, too. Being asleep, or at least having our eyes closed, meant less danger of anyone trying to strike up a conversation.

At last we jolted to a halt, well inside the Third Reich.

'*Dessau, Transit Centre Dessau. Alle bitte austeigen,*' voices were shouting outside. 'Everyone leave the train, please.'

Apparently most transports were first brought to Dessau, which was equipped for delousing and routine medical examinations. Men and women were dealt with separately, grouped into batches of a hundred and then divided again into fifties.

A German civilian took charge of our group of fifty and politely explained that we had been chosen for work in the immense I. G. Farben *Aluminium Werke*, an industrial complex on the outskirts of Bitterfeld, a town halfway between Dessau and Leipzig. A hut had been specially built for us in the grounds of the works.

On arrival we had to write a brief outline of our background so that our jobs could be allocated. Anyone who could speak German was asked to come forward. Out of the fifty of us, only three could do so: my mother, myself, and a Ukrainian girl who didn't seem to belong in our group at all. She really spoke very little German and spoke it badly, but was classified as *Volksdeutsche* – an honour frequently bestowed on supposedly ethnic Germans who in fact were merely willing collaborators – and appointed official interpreter. Unlike the rest of us she did not have to wear a lapel badge bearing a red 'P', which identified Polish slave labourers. This meant she had far more freedom of movement than we did. Right from the start I suspected she had been planted to sort out who was who within the group.

Mother was not taken into the factory but put in charge of the hut, cleaning it and distributing meals, and liaising with the authorities over the girls' welfare. Among the occupants were two pairs of sisters. The paths of Hanka and Genia were to cross mine more than once during ordeals we had not yet dreamt of. Hanka, with whom I struck up an immediate friendship, was dark-haired, rosy-cheeked, and very pretty. Genia was four or five years older and might have belonged to quite a different family with her curly, mousy hair. Of the other sisters, Janka was only about twelve years old and looked much younger. Goodness knows how this pretty fair-haired little creature had been trapped in a labour round-up, unless it was that she had refused to be torn away from her elder sister, Cesia. Poor little Janka was terrified of everything going on around her; she was afraid to go to sleep and cried wretchedly. My mother tried to console her, dressed her in the morning and talked to her, fed her, kept her in the hut all day, saw her into her bunk at night and talked to her . . . kept talking lovingly to her.

In spite of everything my 'aunt', Mrs Sulewska, did on behalf of all the girls, there was resentment. She was older than the rest and would have been incapable of much heavy labour, but still some of the girls were jealous of the fact that she did not actually have to work on the factory floor. Admittedly the work was awful. A lot of it involved shaking out sacks of white powder which went into the processing of aluminium. It stung your skin and made your throat sore; exposure to it for any length of time must have done considerable damage to the lungs.

As for me, I too was spared those miseries. I had not tried to wriggle out of anything, it was just that the German in charge told me that I had been selected for office duties. Nevertheless, the others envied me, as they envied my mother.

At first the prospect of the job was alarming. The rest of the clerical staff was German, and I was to spend every day right in the middle of them. In fact, detection was less likely among the Germans than if I had been working alongside other Polish girls, to whom my accent might have given hints about my origin.

In charge of the office was Herr Meyer, a plump little red-faced man in his fifties who had so far escaped being drafted into the army. Younger men under him were being taken one after the other, which explained why he needed someone like me to take over various administrative duties. Every day when I arrived at work I had to give the compulsory 'Heil Hitler' greeting to my colleagues, which I mentally

followed up with the worst Polish insults I knew. I quickly had to learn
to deal with all kinds of registrations, sick leave procedures, and the
issue of meal vouchers for thousands of workers. These employees
came from all over Europe, some freely, some as slaves. Each nationality and category had a different coloured voucher. Volunteers from
Italy and Hungary who had opted for war work in German industry
rather than military service were provided with better meals and had
their own canteens; volunteer craftsmen from supposedly neutral Spain
also received privileged treatment. Slave labourers were given smaller
rations of poorer quality.

Herr Meyer ordered me to issue myself with a voucher for eating
with the true Reich Germans in their own canteen. It gave me the
shivers, but I was glad of the food. In addition he patiently began to
teach me German shorthand and typing in his own office, and we got
on so well together that one day he let slip a damning confession: he
was secretly learning English, a criminal offence amounting almost to
treason.

After some weeks we were given permission to write and receive
letters, and to receive parcels from home. This was tricky. If my 'aunt'
and I wrote to nobody and received no word and not a single package
from anybody we had left behind, suspicions might be aroused. On
the other hand, if we tried to contact my father what other compli-
cations might arise? In the end we wrote to Father Krasowski and
gave him details of our whereabouts. By then he had heard from my
father, and passed this information on. Soon we had news in return.
At no time did we know my father's assumed name; we wrote to the
peasant farmer at Tarnow who was employing him. Then parcels
began to reach us. Father must have thought we were in a bad way,
for he sent far more than he ought to have done, including packages of
tobacco – most of which I passed on to Herr Meyer, who was delighted,
since this was something the Germans were short of. But such generosity was worrying. Father was alive: we had established that, and it
was enough. A few non-committal letters from time to time would
numb suspicion among the other women. Too many, and too much in
the way of parcels, might do the opposite.

Absurdly, I felt happier and safer when working in the office than
off-duty amongst the other Polish girls. But it was no use trying to
keep to myself. I had to mix. One of the girls I warily learned to trust
was Zosia, with whom I shared a bunk in the hut. She was very bright
and reckless, the sort of tomboy I had once been. We both felt in our
bones that something dreadful was bound to happen soon. We had
reasonable food, we were physically quite well, but the odds were

against us, and if we wanted to be happy we had better try to be happy now, and make every day count. Brazenly we borrowed bicycles from a couple of German girls, took off our 'P' badges and rode about the countryside. It was a region well worth exploring. Sometimes with Zosia and sometimes alone, I used my limited wages to travel by train to Leipzig and Halle, which was of course strictly forbidden. I even went as far afield as the lovely old town of Nordhausen. Here at the foot of the Harz mountains I was reminded of the mountains at home. I could have been such an appreciative tourist if the Nazis had not contaminated their beautiful country.

The Yugoslav slave labourers had their own camp not far from where we lived. It was within the town limits, and provided we did not remove our badges we were allowed to move about in that area. Zosia and I used to walk over to the camp. The men had guitars, and loved to dance and to watch others dance. They, like us, could not board trains or cross frontiers, but they were making the best of a bad job. Parcels from home arrived regularly, most of them with large quantities of slivovitz, so that the evenings usually finished up full of song and laughter. They would gladly barter clothes, food, or whatever came to hand. I was beginning to learn what it could be like to live. Really live, I mean. It could all be such fun. And so easy, if only people didn't spoil things.

One sunny afternoon Zosia and I stopped our bikes by the roadside to admire the spring flowers beginning to show in the grass verges and across the meadow.

'I know what you are,' said Zosia abruptly. 'But don't worry.'

Taken by surprise, I stammered: 'Of course you know who I am. I'm Leokadia, I . . .'

'You're Jewish, aren't you?' Before I could find words or decide what on earth I ought to say, she went on: 'It's all right, I won't give you away. But I'm telling you for your own good that they're after you. That Ukrainian girl, she's been saying there are some Jews amongst us and she's going to dig them out, and she'd better get some co-operation or there'll be trouble.'

It cast a cloud which grew steadily darker. Jolted out of any sense of false security, I watched and listened, keeping constantly alert. I realized that there were in fact several other Jews besides my mother and myself: thirteen all told, according to my reckoning. If just one of us made a mistake, we could all be given away.

One evening when I had taken off my identification badge and slipped into a cinema in the town, I noticed a *Sturmabteilung* (S.A.) man in black shirt, brown uniform and swastika armband sitting right behind me. Just a coincidence. It had to be. But when I left the cinema he kept a few paces behind me. I wanted to run for my life, but made myself walk slowly to show I wasn't the least bit concerned. He followed me as far as the I. G. Farben gates and then turned away.

During the next few days I was on edge, waiting for someone to pounce. Nothing happened. But I stopped my little outings, didn't risk going to the cinema again, and noticed that some of the others were not venturing out as often as before. Mother and I talked together as little as possible, but one afternoon she managed to tell me of a disturbing incident. That morning she had been summoned to the manager's office.

'Mrs Sulewska, I've heard rumours that there are some Jewish girls in your group.'

'Oh, I don't think that's likely,' Mother said.

'Well, you know your people better than I do. Please keep your ears open, and come to me if you suspect anyone.'

Then one girl went missing. We had no way of knowing whether she had been arrested and forced to give away all she knew or guessed about some of us, or whether she had managed to escape altogether. Nor did we dare discuss it, not knowing who was to be trusted. Whatever lay behind the disappearance, surveillance of the whole group increased. You could *feel* it. Mother and I grew more nervous about my father's parcels, especially as he was now hiding letters in them which would have aroused the suspicions of any censor who found and opened one. We tried to find non-committal phrases for our own letters which would warn him off, but they didn't seem to register.

In the office I was still treated in the most friendly fashion. Everybody was so helpful. Even though they must have been taught the official line that all Poles were to be classified as subhuman, I received nothing but kindness. Not just from Herr Meyer; some of the girls slipped me extra titbits of food. I was frightened, and maybe they knew it. Whatever the reason, I shall never forget it. But I still felt sure these days of limited freedom would soon be at an end.

One Friday morning in March 1942 I was busy dating dinner vouchers when the phone rang and Herr Meyer turned to me.

'Leokadia, the chief's on the line. He'd like a word with you in his office.'

This was not unusual. I was often sent for to settle some routine matter. I went off, knocked, and entered the room. Mother was there, along with a few other girls. The expression on her face told me something was terribly wrong. I turned, and there on the other side of the room sat two men. Their peaked caps lay on the table. The skull and crossbones stared me in the face. It was the Gestapo.

Before I could do or say anything, or even think anything, guards tramped along the corridor and pushed more girls in behind me. I had been right. There were twelve of us: everybody I had suspected of being Jewish was there, except the one who had been missing these last few weeks.

Having assembled us in the office, the Gestapo at once herded us out of it again. In deathly silence we were led out of the building to a waiting van and driven off. The rest of them must have been waiting, like me, for something like this to happen; but now that it had we were too stunned to utter a word.

It was a short journey. Within a few minutes we were delivered to Gestapo headquarters in Bitterfeld and taken down a long corridor with small cells on either side. One was occupied. I glanced in – and there was the missing girl, making our total up to thirteen.

We were hustled on. More cell doors were opened. I thought we were going to be split up, but in the end they pushed us all into one cell. The door slammed shut. Hours went by. At last a hulking S.S. wardress came along and opened the door a fraction. Janka was huddled in a corner, crying, with my mother's arm around her. Her sister Cesia said:

'Please, couldn't we have some food?'

'You're not here to eat.'

Interrogation was to come first. One by one the girls were called from the cell to be questioned. None came back.

At last it was my turn. I was escorted into a huge office. At the far end a ginger-haired man wearing rimless glasses sat behind a desk. He was a small man and might have looked insignificant if it had not been for the black peaked cap on the desk, with the skull and crossbones staring at me once again. I felt very cold and shivery. There were several other uniformed men around the room, and a woman sitting behind a typewriter to take down whatever I said. Then I saw that on the desk, close to the ginger man's hand, were all my documents: birth certificate, identity card, ration card, everything.

'What is your name?' His voice was very soft and he spoke very slowly.

'Leokadia Dobrzynska,' I said.

'I mean your real name.'

'Leokadia Dobrzynska. I have no other name.'

Those papers were in order. I was going to stick to the story they told.

He said: 'We must know where you obtained these papers.' His finger was beginning to tap. 'And your real name.'

'But I have no other name,' I said.

'I know you have. You're going to tell me. You're going to tell me everything.'

I said to myself that one thing they must never know was Father Krasowski's part in all this. And they must have no way of tracing my father.

'I can't tell you things I don't know,' I said.

All at once he stood up and thumped his fist on the table. His voice wasn't soft any longer. He was shouting. 'You will tell. You'll tell me everything. But now get out. Go on, out!' He jerked his head at two of the other men. 'Take her away.'

I was taken along the corridor and handed over to the wardress. She pushed me down some steps so that I missed my footing and fell forward. But I picked myself up and didn't make a sound. She shoved me into a cell in the basement and locked me in. The cell had no windows. Just one feeble electric bulb. And there was no bed. I was completely alone.

It was ages before I heard footsteps. The wardress opened the door, and I wondered what I was in for this time. All she said was that it was time to go to the lavatory. She took me there and stood outside on guard.

I still had my gold watch and a couple of smaller pieces my father had insisted on my carrying with me in case of emergency. There was no point in hanging on to them. They would certainly be found and taken from me. So I threw these last souvenirs into the lavatory basin and made sure they were flushed away. Unknown to me at the time, my mother was doing exactly the same thing when taken to the lavatory in another part of the building.

In the back wall of the one I was in there was a small window. Amazingly it was not barred. I was sure it would be possible to wriggle through. But how far would I get? Anyway, I could not leave my mother.

As soon as I emerged I was led back to the interrogation room. The same room, the same man asking exactly the same questions. But this time he appeared more friendly. He produced a box of chocolates such as I had not seen for years, and offered me one.

I shook my head.

'Do you think they're poisoned?' he laughed. 'Look, I'm having one.' He picked one out and popped it into his mouth.

Still I refused.

And still he was in a good humour. 'Come on, you won't see any-thing like this again, not in your lifetime. Have one while there's a chance.'

How true this was. I might as well have one while I was still alive and could enjoy the taste. He seemed in a jovial mood, so I took a chocolate.

'Now,' he said, 'why don't you tell me your name? All your friends have confessed. We know they're Jews, and you're a Jew. Why waste time? Come on and tell me the truth. Your name, for a start.'

'My name is Leokadia Dobrzynska. I can't tell you anything else.'

He walked round the desk, came right up to me and slapped me hard across the face. 'You will. You'll tell me everything else, even if it takes time. Now get out.'

I was put back in my cell, alone, with no idea where anybody was. And then, hours later, not knowing whether it was day or night, I was back in the interrogation room, where Ginger was marching jubilantly up and down with his hands behind his back.

'Well?' he fired at me. 'How would you like to rejoin your mother?'

I felt weak at the knees. I wouldn't let myself collapse, but I was dizzy with fear. How could he have known that my aunt, according to those papers, was my mother?

'Kitty Felix,' he said loudly and triumphantly. 'Kitty Felix. That is so, yes? Your mother has told us everything, so what's the point of being so stubborn?'

I must have passed out. When I came to, in a cell, all the rest of them were there. We were all back together again. Mother was weeping. They had questioned her in just the same way, and she was tricked into believing that I had confessed and told everything. In a weak moment she had thought that I was still not much more than a child, and they could have broken me down, so she confessed our name and our relationship. It had even been hinted to her that I was no longer alive: now she knew, and it was too late. But we agreed never to tell them where the documents had come from. We would never speak. She would never be tricked again. Brave words. But sooner or later, by some means, they would probably get the information out of us.

The following day they had the girls in yet again, one by one. Even little Janka. When my turn came I knew what to expect.

'Where did those documents come from?'

'I don't know. I can't tell you what I don't know.'

He was screaming again. Then he looked round the other men in the room, and laughed, and of course when he laughed they all laughed with him. '*Also morgen gibt es Tanzstunde.*' I could still hear their laughter as I was hustled back to the cell where everyone else was. Late in the day two S.S. men looked in on us. They thought it was a great joke. '*Also morgen gibt es Tanzstunde.* Oh, yes, girls. Tomorrow we have dancing lessons.'

They didn't bother to offer us any food that night. Why bother? Tomorrow we would be dead. It was quite obvious that that was what they had meant.

There was nothing to sit on but the floor. We hunched into corners or sprawled out on the stone flags. Janka crept on to her sister's lap because my mother was occupied with me. No point in pretending any more. We sat close together and she stroked my hair.

One of the girls was sobbing. 'We're going to die tomorrow, they're going to kill us, all of us.'

'Shut up. Do you have to say it out loud?'

The light in the cell was left on. Here, unlike that basement cell where I had been on my own, there was also a skylight. And there was a peephole in the door through which the warders peered from time to time. Some girls dozed off. Others whispered to one another. I crawled across to look up through the skylight and saw the stars. It was only then that it hit me. I would never see the stars again. I began to whimper like so many of the others. Mother came and tugged me away. She made me come back close to her, and right through the night talked on and on to me about my childhood, about my father, about the good times and how really good they had been. I would feel no pain, she promised. It would be so quick and would be over so soon.

'But I don't want to die,' I kept wailing.

I hadn't done anyone any harm. Why should I have to die? Why should anyone in the world want to kill me? It was bad for my mother, but surely it was worse for me: my mother had lived and enjoyed life, she had had some youth and happiness and had been happily married, but what about *me*? Mother made me promise I would be calm and brave. I mustn't cry, mustn't struggle. They mustn't get any pleasure out of killing us, these creatures. I would go out with my head held up. And it had to be the same with the others. She turned to the others and talked to them, telling them the same thing.

Sunrise tinted the skylight very faintly. I'm not trying to write poetically: I can still see the first faint glow of that sunrise.

The cell door crashed open. '*Aufstehen. Alles 'raus, schneller!*'

We were led along the corridor into a courtyard. A row of machine-guns had been set up. So many, to kill so few? There was a thick layer of sawdust along the facing wall – to soak up the blood, so that we didn't make a nasty mess on German property.

'Get to the wall! Face it!'

I tried to give my mother a last kiss, but my head was pushed away by a revolver butt against my temples. We lined up, the thirteen of us, facing those dull, pitted bricks. The last thing we would see on earth. There was a burst of firing, so swift and loud that it was like just one shot and a hundred echoes. As the sound bounced back off the wall and my ears sang with the impact, I instinctively closed my eyes. My first thought was that they had missed me. And the others . . . ?

Everything was silent. Then there was a great roar of laughter.

'Did you really think we were going to shoot you?' Someone was strutting up and down behind us. 'You try to cheat the German Reich and then think you'll be let off that easily? Oh, no. Shooting would be too good for the likes of you. It's a slow death for you, all of you.'

Three girls slumped to the ground. We were made to help them to their feet and support them as we were taken back to the cell. All of us were in tears. But we were still alive.

Within a few hours we were led out to a prison van. A small crowd had gathered. I spotted some of the people I had worked with at the *Aluminium Werke*. Herr Meyer was there, helplessly waving a white handkerchief at me, and he too had tears running down his face. I tried to wave back, but a guard jabbed me painfully in the back to force me into the van.

Once more we were in a train, this time closely guarded. It was a short journey. From Halle station we were marched through the town, with people stopping to stare at us. The first sight of the iron gates of the building for which we were heading made it clear what it was. This was a real prison.

As soon as we were inside we had to queue up for disinfection. Our hair was cropped. We handed in our own clothes and were issued with prison clothes, with numbers sewn on. Then we were fingerprinted, documented, and photographed from three sides with number plates hung round our necks. Obviously we were hardened criminals. And our crime? Being born Jewish.

Now that they had got us shut safely away, there seemed to be no hurry to settle our fate. We had a bowl of soup every day at noon, and at teatime and breakfast bread and cocoa without milk. Once a day we joined other prisoners for exercise in the yard. A wardress stood in the middle while the women plodded round her in a circle. Then the questioning began again. One by one we were taken away from our communal cell, and when my turn came it was always the same: 'Come on, girl, where did you get those papers? We *must* know.'

I think it was then that it dawned on me that Mother and I stood a chance of staying alive as long as we could keep our secret. The methodical Germans wanted a neat and satisfactory answer to their question. While we were still breathing and able to provide it, they would want the annoying gap in their records filled.

Days passed and we lost count of time. In a weird way it was almost a relief to be in prison, not still on the run. We had enough food, even if it was not very good. There was a place to lie down for the night, and our cell was reasonably warm. Even during the repeated interrogation none of us had so far been subjected to any torture.

Then we were all summoned to appear before a sort of court. We were asked the usual questions, one by one, and had to answer in front of all the others. It didn't take long. We were told we had committed a serious crime (apart from being Jewish) by entering the Reich illegally on false documents. This carried the death penalty.

So we were to be executed after all. Soon afterwards we were led out to a huge black car, a sort of Black Maria with an interior divided into small cells – or, rather, cages. The guard told us that we were being transferred to Leipzig prison. I couldn't understand why they should go to all this trouble instead of just shooting us in Halle and being done with it. But then, they still wanted to discover the origin of those documents.

In Leipzig the routine was much as before, though we had a slightly more varied life. Some girls worked in the sewing room, others, including myself, in the kitchens. These activities were always liable to be interrupted by a summons to the interrogation room. The same questions from them, the same blank refusals from us.

Again without warning we were transferred. This time we were despatched to Dresden. Here the prison was quite a modern show-piece, with plenty of glass partitioning, a huge glass roof, and windows all round our large cell. You could actually look out across the roofs of the city. If it hadn't been Cell No. 13 we might have felt positively cheerful.

There were other prisoners already there. They told us this was a transit cell where prisoners were collected until there were enough to make up a transport to a camp at Auschwitz. More than that they didn't know. But we could decipher a few scrawls on the walls of the cell. Among pathetic little poems, names and home addresses were odd messages: *Meet you in Auschwitz . . . On our way to hell . . . If survive, contact so-and-so . . .*

Mother and I were puzzled by this name. We both knew it as the German translation of Oswiecim, a small town in the lowlands some thirty miles north of our home at Bielsko. It stood in a swampy area beside a tributary of the river Vistula, and apart from fishing it had little to commend it. What could anyone be doing up there?

Our cell began to fill up with a mixed lot of prisoners. There were German women serving sentences for murder and other crimes, petty thieves, undesirables who had refused to work hard enough for the Fatherland, and some political prisoners who had spent many years in labour camps. We even had some Russian acrobats, who loved to clear a space and dance and perform in the middle of the floor. I was fascinated. I was no acrobat, but after all the gymnastics I had done in my childhood I was able to join in.

Mother made friends with a German gipsy who had been imprisoned for no other reason than simply being a gipsy. This woman had heard about Auschwitz. There was some sort of camp there where people were kept. Had she learnt this from someone who had come back? No; she had never heard of anyone coming back. Just that there were stories, rumours, a whisper about the place's existence. That was about all.

More and more people arrived. Soon there was no space for acrobatics. Little Janka clung to my mother again. Hanka, the pretty one of the other two sisters, with whom I was striking up a close friendship, went on doing solo dances and singing songs right to the last. 'When I'm out of here,' she used to say, 'when I'm on the stage, when I'm a great star and you all come to see me . . .' Then even she could perform no longer. We were packed in like sardines. Most of us had to stand a large part of the time, taking it in turns to have a brief rest on the floor.

One morning our group of thirteen was called out. I took it for granted there would be another attempt to find out where our forged papers came from. But they were no longer interested.

'We're handing you over to the camp Gestapo. They'll know how to sort you out.'

One by one we were taken into an adjoining office and ordered to sign a form. It was a long sheet and we were not allowed enough time to read it in full, but I could pick out the main points: '. . . endangering the security of the Third Reich . . . had illegally entered Germany with forged papers . . . herewith sentenced to hard labour for life.'

I signed quite happily. We weren't going to be killed, after all. Our sentence had been commuted to hard labour; that wouldn't be pleasant but we could survive it, surely. Anyway it might not be for life, but just until the war was over and we were freed. The official checked my signature and grinned. '*Nun morgen geht es nach Auschwitz.*'

Auschwitz. A work camp. Well, we had heard of those. As long as it was somewhere to live. If there was a camp, there must be people alive in it. We would go, disobey in our hearts, keep ourselves fit somehow, survive somehow. We didn't know much about the work camps, but it couldn't be all that dreadful, this Auschwitz place.

That last night in Dresden prison we experienced our first big air raid. It was nothing like the terrifying destruction which fell on Dresden in the closing stages of the war, but to us it was spectacular enough. From our viewpoint above the city we could see fires breaking out everywhere. All our windows were shattered and the roof was cracked. We cheered wildly. If only a bomb would hit the prison! A bomb just big enough and placed well enough to blow a big hole in the side of the building and let us out.

But the planes went away, and after several hours the fires were put out.

In the morning all the occupants of Cell 13 were taken in small groups down a spiral staircase. I kept at the back of our batch, feeling that my mother was safer in front of me, where I could keep an eye on her. Bringing up the rear was a wardress who looked less of a bully than some of them. I risked asking her: 'This Auschwitz place, what's it really like?'

'It's not for you to ask questions.'

We were loaded into another Black Maria, with all its windows blacked out. When we emerged we found ourselves in a railway siding, beside an enormously long train of smart, newly painted passenger coaches.

'This time we're going to travel in style,' said my mother with the ghost of a laugh.

The windows of the coaches, like those of the prison van, had all been painted over and barred. The interior consisted of a narrow central corridor dividing rows of tiny locked cages. Each cell had been designed for two or four people, but six of us were pushed into one of them. Mother and I managed to stay together. After the cages were filled, the whole coach was shut. It was gloomy and depressing. Individual cells were unlit, and the only illumination came from a dim electric bulb in the corridor ceiling.

Over the next few hours there was a continuous clumping of footsteps outside the train, accompanied by screams and shouted commands. Every now and then a door thumped shut somewhere. Vans or lorries rolled up to the siding and roared away again. Then there would be a period of silence. Then more engines, and more shouts.

We had no food or drink, and there was no one to ask for some. We took it in turns to sit down in the cramped cell. Standing, you had to lean against the wire mesh. My mother was getting very tired, and I

My brother Robert and myself
just before the outbreak of war
in 1939

A room after a destructive S.S. rampage

The Lublin ghetto during an S.S. round-up for deportation

Opposite:
The layout of Birkenau. This plan, drawn immediately after the war by Erich Kulka and presented to the Auschwitz Museum, is used by his kind permission. It shows the functions of Birkenau extermination camp, Auschwitz II, only.

BI was the women's camp which, although much smaller than the men's camp, housed far greater numbers in the most overcrowded conditions. Each short line represents a hut. The top right-hand section was the hospital compound. The *Lagerstrasse* can be seen running right through. The railway line came in through the entrance to the right of the drawing. At the terminal, the crematoria are numbered in Birkenau order: strictly speaking, Crematorium I was in the original base camp of Auschwitz I, a few kilometres away.

BII, the larger area, is the men's compound, sub-divided into various groups such as the hospital block, etc. A section, BIIb, later became part of the women's camp.

The *Kanada* compound is quite separate, marked (g) – BIIg. Lines show the barrack huts. My block was the first opposite the sauna and next to the crematorium. In between were the filter plants where bone ash was filtered to make fertilizer. Beyond Crematorium IV is the path past the sauna, and beyond this line were the pits for burning.

BIII, known as 'Mexico', was never finished.

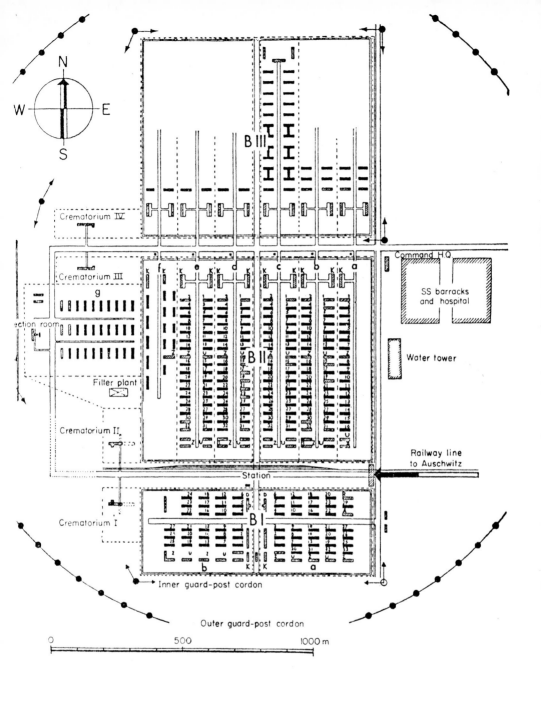

N
W — E
S

BIII

Crematorium IV

Command H.Q.

Crematorium III

SS barracks
and hospital

g

ection room

Water tower

Filter plant

BII

Crematorium II

Railway line
to Auschwitz

Station

Crematorium I

BI

b   a

→ Inner guard-post cordon

Outer guard-post cordon

0   500   1000 m

Arrival of a transport at the Auschwitz ramp (an S.S. photograph)

My mother's Auschwitz tattoo, 39933, and my own, 39934, removed from our forearms after the war and preserved as evidence of the days when we were just nameless numbers in the death camp

tried to push others aside so that she could sit on the floor, which nearly started a row. We had lost touch with our original group, and the other four in our cell were strangers. Two of them were huge Russian women who seemed to be spoiling for a fight. One of them had lost a shoe, blamed the other for stealing it, and set about her in an attempt to kick *her* shoes off. In that confined space we all suffered. Then one of the Russians wanted to go to the toilet. Still there was nobody to ask and no way of getting along the corridor, so she insisted that she would have to make a mess on the floor. We protested and tried to stop her every time she began to squat down. Desperately she hammered on the blank window. But in the end she could hold on no longer and did it all over the floor.

The door at one end of the carriage thudded open. A guard with fixed bayonet stormed along the corridor, wanting to know what all the racket was about. The smell hit him before he reached us. He unlocked the door of our cage, kicked it open, and beat us all about the head, calling us every filthy name he could think of.

One of the women begged for food. 'There's no food here,' was all the answer she got.

It was ages before the train began to move. With no change between darkness and daylight, nothing but that electric bulb feebly on all the time, we had little sense of time and no way of working out how far we travelled.

At last guards came along and escorted women in twos and threes to the toilet. They had left it too late. By now there was mess everywhere.

I was drowsing, propped against the wire mesh, when the train slowed and finally clanked and grated to a halt. The familiar screaming and bellowing started up right away. 'Everybody out. Off the train. Get a move on!'

We scrambled down awkwardly in near-darkness. It was still night, but in the distance was a hint of dawn. There were hundreds of people stumbling about, trying to find their footing on the lumpy ground. We were dazed, unable to get our bearings. Guards moved in, screaming and shoving us into columns. We marched off along the railway line, tripping and lurching as we went. Mother and I stayed side by side.

We came to a gate with a motto above it in iron lettering, silhouetted against the sky: ARBEIT MACHT FREI – Work Brings Freedom. Men who must have been in a different part of the train were taken in through the gate, along with some of the women. It was impossible to make out which women were chosen or why. The rest of us were formed into fives and went staggering on, picking our way with the help of the erratic glare from three layers of illuminated, electrified fencing. Above them stood a rank of high watch-towers.

The railway line petered out. We kept going until we were halted at another gate and a guardhouse. This was in fact the entrance to Auschwitz II, or Birkenau, though at that time we knew nothing of the names or significance of any part of this bewildering place.

A dank chill caught at us. The whole area was shrouded in a clinging grey mist. But dawn was breaking. Or was it really the dawn? A reddish glow through the mist was flickering in the weirdest way, and there was a sickly, fatty, cloying smell. Mother and I glanced at each other, baffled. Who could be roasting meat, great quantities of it, at this hour of the morning?

5

Work Brings Freedom

Whistles screeched suddenly out of the haze, and figures began to pour out of long, low huts in a wild commotion. '*Aufstehen . . . get up.*' The spaces between the huts were seething with people. '*Zählappell. Alles aufstehen zum Zählappell.*' Why on earth was there a roll-call at three or four in the morning?

We stumbled on our way and were driven into a long narrow building which we later heard referred to as the sauna. Women with short hair were pacing up and down, wearing striped jackets and trousers or baggy striped garments which could hardly be described as dresses. Each had a large green triangle on her left breast, identifying her as a German criminal prisoner. There was no uniformed German in sight. These hoarse-voiced prisoners were in charge of lesser prisoners, including newcomers like us; they screamed at us from force of habit, but at first none of the rasping words meant anything.

Mother stepped forward and addressed one of them politely. 'Excuse me, please, but could you tell us –'

'Haven't been here two minutes, and already you want to know so much?' The woman raised a whip. 'You'll learn soon enough.' Then she looked more closely. 'Anyway, what the hell are you doing in this camp, old woman? No room here for old people. Why weren't you sent over there?' She jerked her whip in the direction of that distant glow. 'How did you get in?'

'We've just come from prison,' said my mother. 'Thirteen of us, sentenced to hard labour.'

The woman gaped and looked almost respectful. 'Oh, you must be a political criminal. That's quite different.' It was very confusing. Having a criminal record seemed to put one immediately among the élite in this place. 'They'll be wanting you for questioning, then,' she added with some relish.

We were ordered to strip, and our clothes were thrown into large vats for decontamination. We ourselves were left under a row of cold showers for some time and then dipped in a foul-smelling, bluish-green fluid. While we were still shivering and stinging from this, the *Fryzerki*, the hairdressers, got to work. 'Arms and legs out.' We had to stretch arms and legs wide while they shaved our heads, under our armpits, and between our legs. We looked ridiculous. But even more ridiculous when we were issued with new clothing – if you could call it new. I got a pair of khaki breeches several sizes too large for me, a blouse with odd sleeves, two odd stockings and a pair of clogs. When I turned to look for my mother I couldn't make her out at first and when we did recognize each other we burst out laughing. Both of us looked so clownish. Oh, well – a black sense of humour might stand us in good stead. The uniforms, we discovered later, came from 20,000 Russian prisoners of war who had been massacred just before our arrival.

'*Anstellen, anstellen schneller, verfluchte Bande.*'

We were bullied into a long line and shuffled towards desks where a number of girl clerks sat, looking quite smart and respectable and with longer hair than those we had seen so far. They were methodically taking down particulars of all the *Zugänge*, the newcomers. I was just behind my mother, as usual, and while my documentation was being completed another woman tattooed her forearm. Mother's number was 39933. I became 39934. There was a sharp pain each time the needle dug into the skin. Not knowing anything about tattooing, I thought that when I wanted to I could easily wash the mark off. It didn't occur to me that it was permanent.

The girl tattooing my mother's arm had talked quietly to her as she did so. Had we come here straight from home? Home: the word had ceased to mean anything. Mother explained a few details, and it turned out that the girl was from our own region, not far from Bielsko. She was surprised that anyone of my mother's age had been allowed into this part of the camp instead of going 'over there'. She nodded towards the window.

'What *is* over there?' I asked.

'You'll find out soon enough.'

But the girl promised in an undertone that she would try to help my mother as far as possible. It might be possible to fix her up with work indoors, but not right away: nothing could be done during the six weeks of quarantine. 'I don't know if you'll last out those six weeks. The average life of a prisoner here is about three weeks.'

It was light by the time these procedures had finished. As we left the sauna, I thought I could hear music. I must be dreaming. Music, in this place, at this time of day? But in fact there was a band playing a rousing march at the gate as work parties of women streamed out.

We were told that we would be quarantined in Block 20 of *Lager A* – Camp A. As we were led off we got a full view of this section of Birkenau. Along the centre of Camp A ran a road known as the *Lagerstrasse*. On either side were the blocks: long stone-built huts with only two windows in each. To get to them we had to flounder ankle-deep through mud which clung to our wooden clogs. At the door of our block we were met by a heavily-built woman, well fed and better dressed than those in the sauna but with the same gruff voice. She was boss of the hut, the *Blockälteste* or block senior, and she intended us to understand this right from the start.

'So you're my *Zugänge*.' She put her hands on her wide hips and yelled at us. 'All right, then. Off to the meadow, the lot of you.'

The so-called meadow was a muddy patch of ground, without a blade of grass, at the back of our block. Here we had to spend the day, for no one was allowed inside the hut until night-time. It began to rain, but that made no difference: we were still forbidden to go indoors. We had had nothing to eat or drink since leaving Dresden. One of the girls timidly approached the *Blockälteste*, and was screamed at for her pains. By the time we had gone through decontamination and documentation it had been too late for breakfast here, and that was that.

Settling down drearily into the mud, I noticed some girls peering at us from behind one of the other blocks. After a while a few made their way across to us, and one spoke to me.

'You want to buy a scarf?'

The rag she was holding out would be just the thing to cover my bald, cold head.

'What do you want for it?' I asked.

'Two pieces of bread or one of sausage.'

I told her we'd had no rations at all so far, and asked how she had managed to get the scarf.

'I organized it, of course.'

This was my first encounter with the most important word in the Auschwitz language: 'organization' was the key to survival. It meant to steal, buy, exchange, get hold of. Whatever you wanted, you had to have something to barter for it. Some people spent every waking minute 'organizing': stealing from their fellow prisoners, bribing others, swapping a crust of bread for a can of water, a crumpled sheet of notepaper for a more comfortable corner of a bunk.

It was nearly midday. In the distance we could see big drums being carried out from the kitchens. Soup was on its way. When our cauldron arrived at the block, we were issued with red enamel dishes. One ladle of soup was tipped into each. The smell was awful and the taste was worse. A few bits of potato peel and shreds of swedes floated on top. I tried a mouthful and felt sick, but was much too hungry to leave it.

We all had to drink straight from the bowls. Spoons would have to be 'organized' when we had learnt the ropes.

During the early afternoon more girls ventured over to talk to us. Before we could ask all the questions we wanted to, there was a sudden shout from one of them. 'Run!' They scattered and were gone in a matter of seconds. Instinctively I jumped to my feet and dashed for cover behind one end of the block. Mother moved quickly enough to get to the far end along with half a dozen others. Peeping out I could see a woman approaching, lashing a whip. On her dress was a black triangle, denoting a lower category of German prisoner than the ones wearing a green triangle. Like some demented animal trainer she ran about cracking her whip, rounding up ten newcomers who had not been as quick off the mark as the older hands. Once she had collected these ten she left.

At the end of the afternoon the work parties came dragging back into camp. The band was playing cheerfully again. The women were supposed to pass it at a springy step. But some were falling about helplessly, and at the end of one column I could see three or four life-less bodies being carried in on improvised stretchers.

'*Zählappell. Alles anstellen.*' Shouts resounded through the camp.

This was the evening roll-call. Our *Blockälteste* was immediately all noise and swagger. She flourished her whip, formed us up in front of the block in fives, counted us – and found one missing. Screaming with rage, she went rampaging about until she found a terrified girl cowering behind the block, incapable of getting to her feet. The girl was dragged into place; and the count started all over again. This time the numbers tallied.

And then we stood there in the mud and drizzle. We stood for two hours. One girl fainted. Three more sank to their knees and began to whimper. Then someone in a green uniform appeared on a bicycle at the far end of the *Lagerstrasse*. It was one of the *Aufseherinen*, an S.S. woman.

'*Achtung!*' screamed our *Blockälteste*. The girls who had collapsed were lashed to their feet and forced to stand to attention. The S.S. supervisor dismounted and stalked along the front rank of our platoon, counting each row of five with her stick. When she saw one girl sway, she struck her across the face with the stick. Satisfied that the number was correct, she went off to the main gate. At a special desk there stood a *Rapportführer*, or roll-call leader, an N.C.O. of the S.S., responsible for discipline and keeping count of prisoners throughout the camp. Today the man was the dreaded bully, Taube. I was to see his face again, and suffer the most hideous punishment at his hands.

The number of prisoners, including dead ones, always had to be right. If it was not, there was a recount. Those who died at work or during the protracted roll-call were laid out at the end of a row and included in the count.

As we were at last allowed to inspect our new quarters, one of the block residents said how lucky we had been. Roll-call had taken only two hours. Three to four hours was nothing unusual, she said, and there had been cases of it being prolonged to twelve and even twenty-four hours.

We were anxious to see the interior of our block. At the door, the *Blockälteste*'s assistants handed out evening rations: a few ounces of bread and a tiny smear of margarine. This had to serve as supper and tomorrow's breakfast. Twice a week we might hope to get a small piece of cheese or sausage in addition, unless the privileged prisoners bringing the food from the kitchens stole it on the way.

There were basically two kinds of hut. Some were old wooden stables for army horses, which had been dismantled and brought to Auschwitz in sections for reassembly. Each had a brick heating channel along the middle, and a brick chimney, to keep the horses warm. They had been a privileged class: in Birkenau heating was rarely allowed except in the cosy little office at the end of each block occupied by the *Blockälteste*. On either side of the heating channel were rows of three-tier bunks known as *koje*. Each section of the bunk was enough for one person, but was expected by the camp administrators to hold four or five lying head to toe, and even more when the pace of incoming transports quickened.

The other type of hut was built of stone or brick and had no floor other than the muddy ground, sometimes sticky and sometimes trodden hard, depending on the weather. The bunks were in an almost continuous line, with stretches of permanent planking supported and divided by brick partitions. There were three layers: prisoners who failed to claim a place in a top or middle bunk had to wriggle beneath the lower planks and lie on the mud floor.

In every block, including the sauna, the Germans had painted up encouraging slogans: Love Your Country! Respect Your Superiors;

Be Hard-Working and Obedient; The Block Is Your Home; Cleanliness Aids Good Health; Silence in the Block!

The block was our 'home'. Since we were not supposed to have any personal belongings, there were no lockers or clothes pegs. What you had, you wore. If you took off the garment you had been issued with, it would disappear. Take your clogs off and they would be 'organized'. Apart from that you had little to protect and little to lose, other than a bread ration you might try to keep overnight for the morning. Such refinements as soap and towels were unknown.

On that first night I fought for a place in the *koje*. As a newcomer to a block holding over 800 women, I stood no chance of getting on to the top layer. I squeezed in somehow on the outside of a lower bunk, which meant I had to cling to the edge if I was not to be pushed off. Neither the stinking straw mattress nor the single threadbare blanket reached to where I lay. We were all wet through from the steady rain outside, but none of us dared to undress.

My immediate neighbour was a gipsy who whispered to me that she had got here just two weeks ahead of us. She sounded very strained and feeble, but in the gloom she brought her face close to mine and said:

'I see great strength in your eyes, child. Let me have your palm, and I'll see what is has to say.' She bent closely over it. 'Yes, I can see you *will* come out of here. How, I don't know, but you will be one of the few to see freedom again. Remember, you must never lose your will to live. Fight for your life, or you'll be finished very quickly.'

My first day in Auschwitz was over.

At about four in the morning we were awakened by the deafening shrill of whistles. It was still dark and for a few seconds I hadn't the faintest idea where I was. My cold, damp clothes clung to my skin. Then I recognized the voice of the *Blockälteste* screaming at us to get up. I rolled off the bunk and turned to shake the gipsy. There was no response. She was stone cold and must have died hours before; and I had been lying pressed against her body.

'*Raus, schneller, Zählappell, anstellen.*'

It was time for morning roll-call. On the way out of the block a drink was poured into our bowls. It was a dark, bluish-brown fluid which was probably meant to be tea. The smell was sickening. I tasted it, and it was just as awful as the soup had been yesterday. Nearby, a few of the girls were having a debate. 'Do you think we should drink ours today, or shall we wash with it this time?' Finally they drank one bowl between them, and washed with the rest. They warned me that drinking too much of the stuff was bound to cause diarrhoea.

Last night I had tucked a small crust of bread into my sagging blouse.

It was gone: either it had fallen out during the night or it had been stolen. I ran back to my bunk to look for it. It wasn't there. But the dead gipsy still lay there, so I searched her and found several rations of bread hidden away. I hesitated for a moment; then helped myself to the bread and to her shirt, which was less rough than my ex-army garment and could be worn underneath without showing. This was the first time I had ever taken from the dead. It wouldn't be the last.

Outside I joined the turmoil of women milling to and fro. This was the time of day to make a dash for the lavatory pit – if you could get near it. There were a few buckets in the hut, but they had been filled to overflowing during the night, and a lot of the inmates had messed on the floor.

The roll-call last night had taught me one thing – when the rows formed up it was best to fight your way into the middle. In there you stood less chance of being casually whipped or clubbed by the *Blockälteste* and her subordinates, or by the S.S. supervisor as she checked the final count with her stick. Those in the front row and at the sides got the worst of it. There was a lot to learn, and survival depended on it.

During the quarantine period you were at everyone's mercy. For six weeks you were on the slave market. Locked out of the hut after roll-call, you spent the day on that grassless meadow until someone came hunting victims for a work party. Ten, twenty, one hundred might be needed to dig trenches or pits, to lay roads or work on the railway line. You tried to hide behind the block, or run round the buildings. They kept chasing you with their whips, and would not rest until the requisite number had been rounded up. Then, once the party had been marched off, screamed at and beaten most of the way, you could relax . . . until the next raid.

It was during these six weeks that many of the *Zugänge* died, usually from shock. Large numbers of them from foreign countries had been literally seized in their homes, transported in appalling conditions to this distant camp, and thrown into the horror of it without warning. Mother and I had gone through what you might call an apprenticeship, on the run, in the ghetto, and in prison. Nothing could ever again take us entirely by surprise. We were hardened by now. But not so the dazed, stricken Jews of remoter lands. They went down like flies, dying of shock, dysentery, or typhus, which always raged through the camp. It was particularly bad for those who arrived in winter from warmer climates: Greek girls brought from the warmth of their own country into the middle of a Polish winter stood no chance in this marshy and misty lowland.

Those who were sharp enough to adjust quickly and seize whatever chances were going did find ways of easing their lot. Here and there, in various jobs, reasonably dressed girls were working in what seemed tolerable conditions. There was obviously a way of climbing up through the camp hierarchy, but nobody was going to tell you how. I saw that I had to conserve my energies and wait for an opportunity to get out of the slave market and into a position of responsibility, not much at first, maybe, but with a chance of advancement. But it must be done without hurting anyone else.

Promotion was much easier if you could prove yourself a bully and a willing murderer along Nazi lines. Most of the great complex of Auschwitz and Birkenau camps was in fact run by the prisoners themselves, and it was hideous to see how readily one of your own people would turn against you in return for a few privileges and the chance of a few more months of life. Some were as proud of their armbands, which denoted their status, as of a military decoration, and appeared genuinely touched when they got a word of commendation from an S.S. officer. They set themselves to making careers within the camp, and were very conscious of their status.

The vast majority of prisoners were under supervision all the time, but not always by the people you expected. Nobody was to be trusted: anyone could be a thief, a murderer, a traitor, a spy. Everywhere, all the time, prisoners were to be found aping our oppressors. Every block had its *Blockälteste*, herself a prisoner, and above her was the leading prisoner or *Lagerälteste*. Every work party had its *Kapo* (from the Italian *Capo*, or head), quite possibly a fellow Pole and Jew, who showed her admiration for German discipline by whipping and kicking you. She in turn was fawned on by her *Unterkapo* and *Vorarbeiter*, or leading worker, who could expect promotion if they were assiduous enough in beating up their fellow inmates. Other trusties included the camp police, made up exclusively of Reich German criminals, who were even prouder of their status: no matter what his criminal record, a Reich German was obviously superior to the lesser races, who deserved all they got.

Anybody might attack you and beat you up, and indeed it was expected of the prisoner officials. You had to be on the lookout the whole time. Every minute of the day you had to be on your guard, thinking 'I must get over there . . . mustn't stay here . . .' You had to sense from which direction trouble was coming, and make sure you weren't on the scene when it arrived. That was the key to survival: to be somewhere else . . . to be *invisible*.

Some were lucky and had unexpected opportunities thrust upon them. In her memoirs of the Auschwitz orchestra the singer Fania Fénelon tells about being taken out of quarantine and installed in comfortable quarters with nice clothes simply because a 'Madame Butterfly' was needed for a concert. An S.S. woman swaggered into our own quarantine block and shouted: 'Can anyone here speak German?' Several hands went up. One girl was chosen and led off to become a messenger girl, which put her at once on a privileged level.

I knew someone else who became a messenger girl very early on. It was little Janka. Children were not usually admitted into the camp, but this twelve-year-old, like the rest of us, was somewhat special, having a record as a political criminal. Jewish or not, we had somehow been 'processed' in a different way by the meticulous organizers. Within ten days or so of our arrival Janka was picked out and, as she began to make a fuss about being taken away, her sister was taken along as well. At first the rest of our original group of thirteen were unable to guess what had happened to them, and already we knew better than to ask.

Then we saw them again. Janka had been smartly dressed, she had been allowed to grow her hair again, and looked very pretty and well pleased with herself: they had made her a messenger girl. There she was standing happily at the gate beside an S.S. man as the work parties went out.

Janka had managed to get her sister Cesia a job as block senior. Although Cesia could not have been more than sixteen, she soon became adept at beating up her fellow prisoners. One day, worried about my mother's health and the inadequate rations she was getting, I approached Cesia as an old friend.

'Do you think you could help us?'

She backed away as if from some contagious disease. 'Don't you dare come near me,' she shouted.

'Cesia, surely you remember – '

'One step nearer, and I'll beat you up.'

I couldn't believe she had sold out so soon. 'Have you forgotten my mother? After all she did for you and Janka?' She hesitated, then threw me a hunk of bread. 'Now be off with you. And don't ever dare speak to me again.'

As a counter to such self-seeking treachery little 'families' formed within a block: three or four friends would stick together and organize things together. One acquired some bread, another found a handkerchief or a pencil and some scraps of paper, another a mug of water. Members of a group helped each other and defied the rest. Outside the family there had to be bribery; within there was love and mutual help.

At the end of our quarantine period we were told that the whole block was to be transferred to Camp BIIb and that we were to be assigned to *Aussenarbeit*, outside work. Before this happened, the girl from the reception office who had promised to help my mother proved as good as her word and came to collect her. Mother was allocated to the *Revier*, the hospital compound, which meant better living conditions and escape from the ordeal of hard labour out of doors. Already she had won the younger women's respect. It was unheard-of for anyone of her age to survive the first selection, and she became quite a celebrity. The girls felt protective, those in good work parties such as the offices and kitchens did her little favours, and in the hospital she had the chance to do good work on behalf of others.

The daily ration of food, even if you got it in full, was far less than half what an ordinary human being needs just to exist, without doing a stroke of even the lightest manual labour. To be on *Aussenarbeit*, breaking stones, laying roads or railway track, was to invite early death, especially in winter.

Now that quarantine was ended, I was about to find out for myself what outside work was like. We were divided up into work parties of about 200 and marched out to the sound of the band. At the gate, near the green S.S. hut, stood a group of S.S. women watching us. But we were forbidden even to glance at them.

'Be sure to use your left foot as you go through the gate,' warned the *Kapo*, 'and don't turn your heads.'

We were through. For miles we marched. An hour, two hours, seeing nothing but the vast stretch of the camp until we came to fields and deserted farmhouses; all the little villages and farms in the region had been evacuated. Auschwitz camp wanted no curious neighbours.

When we stopped, we thought we would have a brief rest after that painful tramp in our clogs, but at one side of the road was a heap of huge stones and these had to be carried to a spot much further on, where another work detail was breaking them up for road-building. I stared. Lifting any one of them would be beyond me, let alone carrying it any distance.

'*Schneller, du Arschloch.*' The *Kapo* gave me a jab in the back.

I stooped and tried to lift a stone: it wouldn't budge. As the other girls tugged away and stones from the top of the mound began to crash down, I looked for the smallest. But they were all enormous. With an effort I got one up into my arms and tottered away with it. After three trips, I was finished. My back felt as if it was breaking and

I had a pain in my stomach. Not the ache of a twisted muscle, but the sickening wrench of diarrhoea. My guts were going to drop out. And they did – or at any rate, a filthy mess ran down my legs. That was another of the things you had to get used to if you worked so many hours a day and were beaten up so often. And beaten up I was. As soon as I faltered, an S.S. woman with a dog came racing towards me.

'*Komm schon du verstunkene alte Zitrone!*' Her whip lashed the edge of my cheek. She kicked me in the back as I went down, and there was a pain through my wrist as her Alsatian dog sank its teeth into me. A stinking old lemon – yes, already I was probably that. A few more days of this, and I wasn't sure I'd live to be very much older.

Yet I did live. I worked on *Aussenarbeit* for weeks on end, whipped and kicked by the women and bitten by the savagely trained dogs. Hunger gave us all stomach cramps; the food made us ill. But it was essential not to lose the will to go on: giving up was the first step to self-destruction.

There were girls in our block who worked in a potato field. I decided to try my luck, dodge one work party and attach myself to another, and smuggle in with the farm contingent. It worked. Digging potatoes was not so arduous, and the first day I was able to smuggle two potatoes back into camp, one under each armpit. Now, if only I could organize myself a coat, the floppier the better, it would be possible to carry even more potatoes in the hem and up the sleeves. To manage this I didn't eat any of the potatoes for a while, brought lots of them in, and then at last exchanged them for a ragged old coat. I now had the means for bringing in larger quantities all at one go.

Cooking was something else which had to be organized. Wood had to be found to light a fire in the stove, and water in which to cook the potatoes. With all the restrictions and so many treacherous prowlers ready to betray you, it was only possible to make the attempt after dark when all was quiet. Even then there was a risk. But a few of the other girls brought in some carrots, and we started a fire and so managed the occasional feast of half-cooked vegetables.

I had another use for potatoes. With a couple of them, or with a piece of bread or anything else I could organize, I used to bribe my way into the hospital compound for rare visits to my mother.

Very early on, Mother and I had agreed that no matter what happened, we would not play the Nazi game. Life in Auschwitz was a matter of organizing, of grabbing the bare necessities wherever you could find them. But we would never let ourselves be demoralized into cheating the living. If we took anything, it must be from the dead. People today may flinch from such an idea. But what use had the dead for their clothes or their pitiful rations? Mother, in hospital, had plenty of opportunities for taking bread and the occasional slice of cheese or salami from a corpse; the body suffered no extra misery. To rob the living, or the half-living, was to speed them on their way to death. To organize the relics of the dead was to acquire material which helped keep the living alive, and keep the half-living breathing, with just enough strength maybe to survive until the gates opened on to a freer, sweeter world outside.

A long period of *Aussenarbeit* meant death. I was still sticking it out, but even the farm work was becoming a crippling ordeal as the late summer grew hotter, and what had once been wearisome mud turned into hard ruts and furrows in which you could easily break a leg.

One day I was not quick or cunning enough to dodge a *Kapo* on the hunt, and was dragged into a railway line *Kommando*. Prisoner work parties, whether out in the fields or on specific jobs within sections of the camp, were known as *Kommandos*. At the time of our arrival the railway line did not reach the main entrance of Birkenau. Now it was being hurriedly extended right up to new buildings and chimneys.

I remember, as clearly as if it were yesterday, that *Lagerführerin* Mandel was at the gate with her subordinates that morning. She was S.S. commandant of all the women's camps at Auschwitz from beginning to end, an extremely smart and beautiful woman. In later years I was to learn from other survivors' memoirs that she often took a sentimental fancy to a woman prisoner and would treat her as a pet until she tired of her; then she would send the woman to her death. These attachments were never, of course, to Jewish prisoners: Jewish men and women were not fit to be touched by the Master Race, except in routine beating and killing.

'Look ahead!'

We marched to the beat of the orchestra, all aware of Mandel and her pack as we approached, but nobody daring the slightest glance sideways. Anyone who risked an 'eyes left' would be pulled out and never seen again. *Kapos* marched in front, with the deputies known as *Anweiserinen* at the sides to make sure no one got out of line, and an armed S.S. guard or *Posten* bringing up the rear.

We reached the site. In the distance groups of men were humping cement and beginning to erect some huts. We stared at them, trying to make out faces and wondering who they were, where they had come from, how long they had been in captivity. But we did not dare shout or wave.

'Right, here we are.' Our *Kapo* struck the ground with her stick. 'Start digging. Along this line.'

We had to dig a long trench. I had no idea what it was for. The sun was beating down and the bogland was parched. I couldn't have been caught at a worse time. Only the night before I had traded in my scarf for a place to lie down, and now my head had no protection against the scorching heat.

We were issued with heavy spades. I leaned on mine, got my foot on it, and tried to push it into the ground. All I achieved was a slight scratch on the iron-hard surface. It was impossible to cut through the solid crust, let alone dig any soil out. None of us had the physical strength any more for that sort of task. I cursed myself for not managing to evade this *Kommando*. Digging trenches might seem easier than humping huge stones, but in this sort of weather it certainly was not.

The *Kapos* all along the various groups were enraged when they saw that no progress was being made. Their *Unterkapos* and *Anweiserinen* came screaming in with their sticks, hitting and kicking and swearing. Didn't we realize the S.S. women would soon be here for their usual inspection? 'And you scum, you haven't even scratched the surface!'

I stood on my spade and tried again to drive it down.

'That's not good enough,' yelled one of the assistants.

I couldn't take it. 'Why don't *you* try?' I cried back at her.

The *Kapo* standing close by hit me full across the face. As I swayed, one of the other girls in the party came up beside me, and the two of us set our feet to the spade. We drove hard down, and this time cut through. Some bits of soil came up. The *Kapo* and the *Anweiserinen* snarled, but left us to it and went off to seek other victims.

Once through the dry crust and into the moister soil, we were able to make some progress. But we didn't rush it. The moment we were sure our watchers were a fair distance away and otherwise occupied we rested on our spades until they turned back. To and fro they went, making sure the holes were growing larger, while we kept work to a minimum.

By ten o'clock, having left the camp at about six, we felt as if we had done a full day's work. The sun grew hotter. Some of the girls collapsed under showers of blows. There was nowhere to shelter, even if we had been allowed a rest. On that whole stretch of land there was only one bush, and under it was the S.S. *Posten*, settled drowsily beside his gun, lazy and content to leave the supervision and bullying to the *Kapos* and their team.

Whistles blew. It was midday. At last we were allowed to sit down. Even then it all had to be done by numbers. We sat in groups of five and were not allowed to move. Huge cauldrons of soup were carted on to the field. There was some delay before we got it, as a row broke out between *Kapos* of the different sections: a couple of them swore they were not getting the proper rations for their group, and accused the women who had brought the soup of helping themselves between the kitchens and the site. It would have been nice to think the *Kapos* were concerned for our welfare, but in fact it was just another example of their own battle for power, each one trying to be more assertive than her neighbour. When it came to stealing, they themselves were in the top class.

When the lid of our cauldron came off the nauseating smell reached us from yards away. But we were desperate for some kind of food. This time the soup was made of nettles, with some green and yellow bits floating on top. Possibly there were some lumps of stringy meat and some potato thickening; but the *Kapos* refused to stir the soup, leaving anything of that kind at the bottom for themselves. Ladles of the thin liquid were poured into bowls, which were brought round to us. Those with previous experience tried to sit down with a group of five a good way from the cauldrons, in the hope that as the level sank they would stand a chance of getting something just a bit more substantial.

If the *Kapo* thought you had worked well, you might get a slightly larger helping. A punishment might be no soup at all. I was lucky to get anything. It amounted to no more than a few mouthfuls, but even then I had to hold my nose before I could swallow it.

It was made clear to us that we ought to count ourselves lucky. Some work parties got no midday meal at all when on *Aussenarbeit*: their soup was tipped into bowls in their block, back in the camp, and left there to get cold until they were finally allowed indoors at night.

After swallowing the nettle liquid, we were given a couple of minutes to go to the toilet before resuming work. When I say 'go to the toilet' I mean that we were allowed to move a few yards away and squat down in the field, in full view of one another. Later in the afternoon there was every chance that the soup would have its effect and make you foul yourself while still digging; you would not be allowed to stop then.

Whistles ordered us back for the afternoon session. I tackled my hole again, lifting the spade and putting it down, exercising the spade and myself as little as possible. Later there was a roaring and sputtering noise in the distance. An S.S. man on a motorcycle came bumping from the camp along the edge of the field, followed by an S.S. woman with two dogs on long leashes. They had come to inspect progress. When the woman reached me, she glared into the hole at my feet. 'Swine! Is this all you've done?' A blow over my head with her whip knocked me to my knees. The dogs growled approval. Then, as they moved on to the next girl down the line, our *Kapo* hurried up with an obsequious whine, waving her arm at me. 'Oh, we know this one. She doesn't like work. She asked *me* to dig.' The S.S. woman turned back and set about me again, until I was crumpled on the ground. 'Pick yourself up,' she screamed at last, 'and get on with it, if you want to see the camp tonight.'

When the inspection party had gone you could almost feel the sigh of relief, like a faint breeze across the sweltering field. I leaned on my spade for a few minutes. A group of men were shambling past, hauling and pushing carts of cement. They came so close that we couldn't resist shouting at them.

'Where are you from? Warsaw, Cracow . . . ?'

'Anyone there from Poznan?'

'From Lublin . . . ?'

A couple of skinny arms waved. One man called back: 'Someone from Lublin in the party over there, on the other side. Or caught somewhere near Lublin.'

The *Kapos* started racing about to shut us up. The *Posten* sat up and threatened us with his rifle. But covertly we watched the next column that was straggling towards us. They passed quite close, too, manhandling a cart over the ruts. In the middle of those bowed heads I thought I glimpsed a face I knew, but couldn't think who it would be.

'Anyone from near Lublin?' I cried out.

'Over here.'

His face turned towards me, staring, without a flicker of recognition. It was my boy-friend Simon, from Zabia Wola.

'Don't you remember?' I called. But then I realized how like all the rest of them I must look, after these four months in the camp, with a shaven head and prison clothes. 'Kitty. I'm Kitty.'

He muttered something, and looked stricken.

'Where are you?' I asked, even though the *Kapo* was lumbering across the ruts in my direction. It was too much to hope she would trip and break her ankle.

He was in Birkenau BII, just across the fence from us. That was all we had time to find out.

All day I had been telling myself I must wriggle out of this work detail as soon as possible. Now I knew I had to stay on it, to see him again and find out if there was any way of making real contact.

By the end of the afternoon, many of the girls had collapsed; scores were unconscious on the ground as the whistles blew for our return to camp, and the rest of us, in not much better shape, had to drag them along or improvise stretchers from the building material on the edge of the men's work site.

We approached the gate shuffling and stumbling, but the moment we heard the band we had to straighten up and march with knees lifted high to the beat of the music. Again we were counted to make sure that the same number came back as had gone out. And then there was a commotion, rushing to and fro, getting ready for the block roll-call, being counted again. Not all of us were on our feet now. Those who lay on the ground still breathing, and incapable of getting up even when kicked and beaten, ran the risk of being declared unfit for further work and taken away. You didn't ask where. Those who were dead were piled up in heaps ready for collection by cart or, if there were a lot of them, by tip-up lorry.

It took me weeks to find a way of communicating with Simon. Our work parties were kept further apart, and besides that, I doubted whether I would be able to last much longer on that outside labour. When I did manage to get word through to him, it was because I had also managed to get myself left behind when the work parties marched out.

I had already grasped the value of being invisible. Not being around when the hunters came. Having an unidentifiable face. There were thousands and thousands of women in the various sections of the camp, and even the *Kapos* were unable to tell one from another. With shaven heads, ravaged faces and ill-fitting garments, everybody looked so much alike. That was part of the Nazi plan, after all: to reduce all of us to impersonal, downtrodden nothingness. Even a *Blockälteste* could have up to 1,000 women in her hut, and the continually shifting population made it impossible for her to pick out any individual unless there had been some breach of regulations and she needed a scapegoat. As long as numbers tallied, nobody cared about faces.

It was strictly forbidden to move from one block to another. Social calls were not encouraged in Auschwitz. Friends disappeared, and you had no way of looking for them or saying goodbye. If you had been parted from a sister, cousin or friend, you stayed parted. Yet people did dodge between blocks and make contact. It was dangerous, but then everything in that place was dangerous. You could be beaten to death if caught; but you could be beaten to death for almost anything, so it was up to you to decide which risks to avoid and which to take.

The time for visiting or snatching a few precious minutes of conversation was during the commotion before roll-call. Everyone rushed about then. When the whistles went, some rushed for the lavatory pit, others huddled in a corner to do their bit of bartering and organizing, and some took the chance of crossing to another hut. The general confusion could last for up to an hour, with whistles shrilling and every petty criminal with an armband yelling and cursing at random.

If you ventured too far afield there was the danger of finding yourself on the wrong block when the S.S. at last came in and everyone was called to attention. Many were so ill and confused, on the verge of dying, that they might blunder into the wrong line-up anyway. This was one reason why roll-call could take so long. A *Blockälteste* with several women too many would hide the extra number away in the hut. But if she was short there would be outbreaks of rage and a wild hunt all over the place. If you did find yourself trapped in another block's roll-call, you stayed put and hoped the figures would balance out.

I had noticed that a large number of girls in the block next to ours worked on a special *Kommando* distinguished by red scarves. After inquiry I found they worked at the Siemens factory which had been built outside Auschwitz to make the most of slave labour. They were divided into a day shift and a night shift, which meant that there would be prisoners allowed to sleep inside during the day, unlike most of the other blocks. Now I knew what I had to do.

My first step was to organize similar clothes. Their striped dresses were noticeably different from the sort I had been issued with, and I didn't possess a red scarf. So it was back to my old contacts in the potato fields. Once I had smuggled enough produce into the camp, the dress and scarf were soon forthcoming. Then one morning I hung about as the night shift came off duty, slipped into their ranks as they collected their rations and went on with them through the doorway of the block. Nobody spotted me. They were all too exhausted, thinking only of a few bites to eat and then some hours of sleep. I wriggled with the others into the *koje* and settled down, then got back to my own block for the evening *Zählappell* and the distribution of our bread ration before going to bed for the night. In this way I managed double rations, lots of sleep, and no work to wear me out. Above all I was not exposed to the random beatings of *Kapos* or S.S. guards.

Of course I did not sleep the entire time. And it was while lying awake one afternoon that a chance arose to pass a message through to Simon. No communication was permitted between the men's camp at Birkenau and the women's. But routine maintenance had to be done in both camps, and this was a job for skilled men. There were plenty of trained electricians, carpenters and general repair men in the camp, and some enjoyed an easier life than their fellows and undoubtedly an easier time than the inmates of the women's camp.

I had been watching a number of these men during the hours I was supposed to be asleep, and saw things which I did not understand. I had been puzzled before by the behaviour towards each other of some of the women. It was common to see a couple of girls sitting on their bunks delousing each other; years later, whenever I went to the zoo with my children and saw monkeys picking nits off each other, I was reminded of my friends in Auschwitz. But I didn't understand them stroking, caressing, and murmuring to each other. This did not happen often, because they were usually too tired. But every now and then this hunger for physical contact was greater than their weariness. It all looked so silly, the hurried undressing and fumbling. And now, even more perplexing, came the intrusion of the men. One day one of them took the *Blockälteste* into a corner – sex in full view, if anyone other than myself had been awake or could be bothered to watch. By the nature of their jobs both the man and the *Blockälteste* were privileged prisoners, otherwise they would not have had the strength for sex. It was all over in a few minutes. A chunk of bread changed hands, and that was the end of it.

My chance to get a message to Simon came when two men arrived one day to fix a hinge or something in the door of the block. Everyone except me was asleep and too tired to be woken by any noise the workmen might make. One turned round, noticed that my eyes were open and gave me a tired, friendly grin. I slid off the bunk and began whispering to the two of them. They knew which block Simon would be in but didn't know him personally. By a stroke of luck, however, his particular section had quite a decent *Unterkapo*, and it was just possible I would be allowed to get a message through – provided, of course, that I had some bread or a few slices of salami.

The men promised they would be back next day. They were in no hurry to finish their easy job and be put on something worse. When I saw them again I had organized a scrap of paper and a stub of pencil, and wrote a few words to cheer Simon up. I got a message back from him. It said very little. Either he was afraid of the note falling into the wrong hands, or he was too despondent to make much effort.

We kept up a spasmodic correspondence for a few weeks. I had to pay with bread and other rations from the dead, smuggled out of the hospital compound where my mother worked. She organized enough for me to pay the messengers and even pass a few scraps to Simon. But the few sentences he sent me were becoming more and more wretched. He couldn't hold out. What was the point of trying?

The *Unterkapo* went further than one would have expected in helping Simon. He got him into an indoor weaving detail. But still I received dispiriting messages. One day I risked getting close enough to call across to him, and he tried to say something cheerful back. But he hardly seemed to care. In my next note I said that he was alive today, and must decide to be alive tomorrow, and not think any further ahead than that. Then some weeks passed before I could get another glimpse of him. What I saw told me at once that he was doomed. His shoulders sagged, his eyes were sunken, and he shuffled along without any sense of direction; his arms were skeletal, his head was a loosely wagging skull: he had become a *Muselmann*.

Nobody seems quite sure how or why this term, the German for Muslim, came to be part of camp jargon. It meant a prisoner who had given up hope. When you reached that stage you went downhill fast. A bleary look came into your eyes, your feet dragged, and even when they managed to shuffle you along they had no conscious destination. Even food, the obsession of every living being in the camp, ceased to matter. Complete physical and mental disintegration was close.

The men or women who gave up soonest were not always the ones you might have predicted. It had nothing to do with social background, intellect, or even religious belief. You might think an intellectual ought to have been able to cope better than a bewildered peasant, but it was often the other way round. The well-educated man, in good health and with a clear mind when he was thrown into the camp, tried to find some rational, philosophical way of coping with the incredible situation; and just because it was so foul and incredible, his mind cracked and surrendered. Those of us who had been gradually conditioned to what lay in store, and who kept our eyes fixed only on our fundamental day-to-day existence, were hardier. Insensitive, if you like. Sensitivity was something you had to stow away for the duration.

Mother would try to grab any *Muselmann* who shambled past, offering food and talk. She would keep on talking, try to shake them out of their trance, persuade them it wasn't all over yet, they had to keep going. In hospital she talked to women whose blank eyes showed they had given up. By then it was usually too late. A few could drag themselves back, especially if their despair had been largely caused by illness and now they were recovering. But most no longer had the will. Even when set upon by guards and dogs, a *Muselmann* hardly bothered to dodge. Nor did they have the desperate energy to take the way out that so many men and women chose: by throwing themselves on to the electrified fence. The camp was ringed and criss-crossed with these deadly wires, and it was forbidden to go anywhere near them. Furious with anyone who tried to abandon life in this way, the S.S. would shoot if you made the slightest move to cross the ditch within the perimeter of the fences. If we were to be killed, it had to be in their time and at their pleasure, in no circumstances at our own.

Simon disappeared from the scene. The last news I had of him came in a roundabout way through my mother, who heard that he had been admitted to the men's hospital compound. Like so many enfeebled prisoners, he had contracted typhus and was sent to the infirmary, less for his own benefit than to stop infection spreading through his block. There he gave up and died.

His existence had given me something to hang on to for a little while. I had persuaded myself that in some way I was helping him, and this helped me too. Now I no longer had even that tiny illusion to cling to. When I look back I wonder if there was ever any hope of saving him. Anyway, what I'd attempted had not been enough, and now he was gone.

It was around this time that I learnt you really can go on without any expectations at all: just the sheer refusal to be defeated, saying to yourself over and over, no, no, *no*. It was only a follow-up to what I had instinctively worked out for myself when we were on the run: food, sleep, shit.

Shifting shit was one of my happier jobs in the camp. It was a great step up in the Auschwitz world when I was drafted into the *Scheisskommando*. When we arrived at the camp there had been few separate toilet buildings. When you wanted to shit, you sat precariously balanced on boulders above a deep, stinking pit. It was all too easy to fall in and drown. But then, as well as the lavatory huts for privileged prisoners, the authorities authorized four new lavatory blocks at the rear of the camp. Again, this was probably not for the inmates' comfort: the spread of disease was becoming so alarming that for their own sake they had to attempt some controllable form of sanitation. Each of the specially constructed lavatory huts had a long row of slightly raised concrete with holes, like some sort of misshapen bagatelle board. They provided a wonderful new meeting-place. If you could find one of your friends during a roll-call commotion, you could sit sharing a hole and talk for as long as you dared. As a matter of course there was a guard at the door to hit you going in and coming out. But it was worth it. In the *Scheisskommando*, digging out the mess from underneath and carrying it away in buckets on a yoke across my shoulders to be dumped in pits, I had the privilege of frequent access to the toilets. This meant twenty times the conversation and organizing I'd been able to manage up till now.

In a sudden surge of 'cleanliness is next to godliness' enthusiasm, the authorities next decreed the construction of washrooms. Months had gone by since I had last washed in water – we all made do with our undrinkable tea – and the prospect was delightful. But the *Waschraum*, which had real taps, produced only trickles of marshy water, there were hundreds of women to those few taps, and ordinary prisoners stood precious little chance of getting to them. You needed an armband and a stick to be sure of your place in the queue. Some girls washed in their own urine, having read in some magazine in the distant past that it was good for the complexion. And it was supposed to be a disinfectant.

My own skin had become a mixture of dark grey and red. It was quite impossible to kill all the lice that overran every inch of human skin, forming crusts, especially on the scalp. As with many other things in those cramped conditions, you became obsessed by them. You tried to cope with your own fleas and lice, and took a sort of family pride in them at the same time as hating them. Other people's lice were even more hateful, particularly when they tried to shift over on to you. They dug under the skin, and it was impossible to get them out; impossible, too, to keep from scratching, yet that was the worst thing you could do, for when the skin was broken it soon became infected. My whole body was blotched with scabs and boils, especially on my legs, which oozed pus. After a while I ceased to notice that they hurt; I squeezed them out regularly, but they wouldn't heal, and the holes they left got bigger and bigger.

We were rotting to a slow death, just as the S.S. in Bitterfeld had promised. It was impossible to keep the body clean, yet if you failed you were hastening your own death. To have *Krätze* (scabies) or any other obvious infection meant you would be hauled to one side during medical inspection – or selection, as it was called.

'*Lagersperre! Lagersperre!*'

That cry meant we were immediately confined to the block. In the middle of the day it could only mean a selection.

I can still conjure up a picture of the three men striding down the *Lagerstrasse*, accompanied by an armed guard. Those of us who had been inmates long enough recognized all three: Mengele, the S.S. doctor; *Rapportführer* Taube, whom amongst ourselves we derided as the *Abortführer*, Lavatory Leader; and *Lagerführer* Hössler, the S.S. officer in charge of camp discipline. They turned and made their way towards Block 22. Not ours today, thank goodness.

Every one of the women had to strip and parade naked in front of Mengele. In his immaculate white gloves he stood there pointing sometimes to the right, sometimes to the left. Anyone with spots on her body, or anyone whose slumping and shuffling denoted a *Muselmann*, was directed to the right. That meant death. On the left you were allowed to rot a little longer. Out of 400 girls parading before him that day, Mengele chose 320 to die.

They were taken to Block 25. That was a place nobody ever dared go near, and we gave it a wide berth even when it was empty. Once the naked girls had been driven in, the doors were bolted and the windows barred, and they were kept there for two or three days without food or water. All through those days and nights you could hear screams and sobbing, and an occasional snatch of prayers and singing. Hands stretched through the bars begging for a sip of water. But it was out of bounds.

Usually lorries came to take the victims away. This time they failed to arrive. At the end of the fourth day the S.S. men opened the doors. The smell made even them jump back. Most of the prisoners were dead, heaped on top of one another. Those still alive were sent back to their block, weeping with relief. Someone had heard a rumour that there were to be no more selections. How foolish it was to believe such tales. Apparently the truth was that the Camp Commandant had not received the usual authorization from Berlin. Soon after the release of the surviving girls it came through, and during the night the lorries came and took them to the gas chambers.

All too soon there was a selection from my own block. Two S.S. women came in, with the *Blockälteste* fawning beside them, and began to write down the tattoo numbers of a random selection of girls. The choice seemed quite arbitrary; you got the impression the S.S. needed a certain quantity, just as for work *Kommandos*, and when they had reached it they would be satisfied.

When they had left, girls whose numbers had been noted down began to cry.

'They're going to kill me,' one screamed over and over again.

We tried to reassure them. It couldn't happen just like that, it was all to do with something else. It had to be.

'They've taken my number, they're going to kill me, I know they are.'

At roll-call the numbers were read out. The girls were taken to Block 25, and after a couple of days the lorries came for them.

Another of the insane, obscene things in the camp was that you were not supposed to know about the gassing or burning. Everybody knew really, yet nobody dared mention it. In a fit of rage some S.S. woman might threaten and wave her arm meaningly towards the distant build-ings and chimneys, and the interminable selections of women to be dragged away and never returned could mean only one thing. Yet at other times even a trusted *Kapo* who had been overheard talking about extermination chambers would herself be shot, beaten to death on the spot, or taken away to be gassed. The same thing would happen immediately to any prisoner of lower standing who even mentioned the subject: you were gassed as punishment for having dared to suggest that any gassing whatsoever was going on!

Every day if you were out of doors you could see trains near the main entrance, where the railway line now reached, tipping out hundreds and hundreds of people. There would be almost unbroken columns of women and children, and sometimes older men and boys, plodding along towards the crematoria. Each group left its luggage behind on the platform, and from those belongings came most of the 'organized' luxuries and extra food in the camp.

With each incoming transport and each internal selection from the camp blocks there would be a build-up of that glow in the sky, and the sickly burning smell would drift across the whole area. Still you were not supposed to refer to it. The S.S. wanted no panic and no stampeding mobs: keep everything tidy, steady and methodical, please.

You didn't want to believe, anyway. Least of all could you accept that it would ever happen to you personally. Perhaps something awful was being done to other people, but you were better off not knowing, or at any rate not being quite sure. I don't think any of the women I knew, even those who were dragged away screaming, ever really accepted the truth of what was waiting for them until they were face to face with it.

Even the Germans had an innocuous way of referring to the matter in their records. 'Selection for special treatment' was the phrase. It sounds almost inviting: as if they were offering a treat rather than 'treatment'. If they had their reasons for pretending even to themselves, then it was only by pretence that the rest of us could hope to stay sane. And maybe stay alive long enough to get out one day and tell the whole world the truth, that what was special about it was that its chief aim was the extermination of the entire Jewish race.

6

The Final Solution

I LIVED through Birkenau without ever understanding how any members of a great nation could not only indulge in such wickedness, but deliberately set about contaminating everyone else. For that was part of their policy: to turn their prisoners into beasts and then turn those beasts against one another. Only afterwards did I read the full history of those years and I still cannot fully understand. As it is barely credible to someone like myself who lived through the worst of it, perhaps I ought not to be surprised at members of a younger generation who cannot believe it happened at all. But I did live through it; and I do know it happened.

In his early twenties in Vienna, Adolf Hitler conceived an irrational hatred of Jews. Like many other German and Austrian soldiers defeated in the First World War, he wanted to find someone to blame for that defeat. Among his scapegoats the Jews took first place, and soon were blamed for everything else that was wrong with the world. Hitler wallowed in the anti-Semitic propaganda of the Austrian press. He saw Jews as begetters of every form of 'filth and profligacy, particularly in cultural life' and of 'the seduction of hundreds of thousands of girls by repulsive, crooked-legged Jew bastards'. He continued to abuse them right up to the last lines written in the Berlin bunker shortly before his suicide. The more humiliations, real or imagined, that he endured in early life, the more his hatred grew against supposedly inferior races. Slavs and Hungarians were among these, but overridingly it was Jews.

From the moment his Nazi party attained power in 1933, Hitler deliberately set out to work off his personal perversities. Jews had to be eliminated not just from every walk of life, but from life itself. As a beginning, they were removed from the civil service, and when the arts and journalism were brought under the Reich Chamber of Culture they were dismissed from theatres, orchestras and publishing houses. The legal and medical professions were purged. Many distinguished scientists, musicians and writers did not wait to be humiliated but fled abroad while there was still time.

In 1935 the Nuremberg Laws deprived all Jews of German citizenship. Their status was reduced to that of a barely tolerated subject class, soon to be slaves – or corpses. The Law for Protection of German Blood and German Honour forbade marriages between 'Aryan' Germans and Jews, and the employment of German servants by Jews. Soon they were banned from any job whatsoever. Shops, restaurants, hotels, cinemas and public transport carried notices forbidding them entrance; park benches bore notices forbidding them to sit down.

The internal affairs of other countries were supposedly none of Hitler's concern. Repeatedly he announced that he had no territorial ambitions in Europe. Then, after snatching a piece of Europe, he would declare with shining sincerity that he had no *further* territorial ambitions in Europe. But as he enlarged his Greater Germany, he gave priority to the destruction of the Jews.

After Austria had been occupied in March 1938, the Nazis and their local sympathizers at once set about insulting the Jewish community. In many ways the local thugs were more vindictive than their new overlords. Jews were made to scrub pavements on their hands and knees to an accompaniment of kicks and jeers from the S.S. and civilian passers-by. Those with enough money to bribe their way out of the country had to pay their last penny into Heydrich's cunningly contrived Office for Jewish Emigration, administered by Adolf Eichmann – himself, like Hitler, an Austrian. Of the rest, thousands were thrown into prison and in due course sent to concentration camps. Many of those who escaped went to Poland. But that country's anti-Semitic tradition was nearly as strong as Germany's, and the Nazis had already set their sights on it.

In 1938 Jews in all territories controlled by Germany were formally denied the right to practise law or medicine, though in effect this had applied in Germany itself for some considerable time already. Jewish members of famous Austrian orchestras were dismissed from their posts.

November 1938 provided an excuse for increased persecution. It was a flimsy one, but by now the Nazis were almost past needing justification for their sadism. A teenage German Jewish refugee in Paris went to the German Embassy intending to shoot the ambassador, but instead killed a third secretary. Under the control of Reinhard Heydrich, Himmler's deputy in the S.S., a 'spontaneous' demonstration was mounted to combat 'the Jewish conspiracy against the German nation'. Jewish homes and shops were attacked, synagogues smashed and burnt, and up to 100 Jews were murdered in one night. Police and fire brigades were instructed not to intervene unless there was danger to neighbouring Aryan property. No official proceedings were taken against known murderers, since they all belonged to the Nazi party and so were above the law. Instead, Heydrich ordered that Jewish property should be seized in reparation for the damage caused, while the Jews themselves were shared out amongst concentration camps that had room for them.

It was soon obvious that if the campaign was to continue there were not enough concentration camps. Something would have to be done.

The earliest camps had been designed largely for political prisoners and critics of Hitler's régime. Immediately after his seizure of power he had issued his *Schutzhaft* (Protective Custody) decree to deal summarily with any active opposition. By 1939 the Nazis had established six concentration camps, each with a capacity of some 20,000. When war broke out and Germany marched into Poland, this accommodation was soon increased.

Before the war these prisons within the Reich were used for 'preventive detention' of dissidents. Once war had begun, the numbers were swollen by Resistance fighters and Jews from occupied countries. Between 1937 and 1945 over 200,000 prisoners were sent to Buchenwald, for example. The number known to have been exterminated there by April 1945, when it was liberated by American forces, was over 56,000, and it was known that around 13,000 had been shipped to subsidiary death camps. For this was what they had speedily become: not merely detention centres but centres of calculated mass execution.

By 1942 Himmler had begun to allow the use of slave labour from the camps in local armaments work, and within a short time the S.S. were leasing factory space to the major German combines. It was agreed that certain types of prisoner could be worked to death and that others were to be used for medical experiments, mostly carried out without anaesthetic. Any brutality shown to such prisoners was excused by Himmler on the grounds that it was 'fighting sub-humanity . . . the best indoctrination on inferior beings and the sub-human races'.

Most of these procedures came under the jurisdiction of the S.S., defined by Hitler as 'a State military police capable of representing and imposing the authority of the Reich within the country in any situation . . . within whose ranks are men of the purest German blood and which identifies itself unreservedly with the principles supporting the greater German Reich'.

In fact, as time went on the S.S. became less pure than the Führer had originally planned. To keep the growing number of concentration camps going, it proved necessary to conscript other administrators. There were foreign volunteers such as those from Spain, and collaborators from occupied countries eager to be classified as *Volksdeutschen*, racial or honorary Germans. Many of them could speak little or no German. They could be far more vicious than the true S.S.; afraid of their superiors, they proved their mettle by showing even greater savagery. It was established that more than 150,000 foreigners served at one time or another with the S.S. But although there were prison camps within Germany staffed by men and women of this kind who enjoyed practising torture and degradation, and although some operated extermination sections, wholesale extermination did not come into its own until the creation of Auschwitz.

Once Poland had been overrun a new site had to be found to house Poles rounded up in mass arrests. It also had to be capable of expansion into a prisoner-of-war camp when the attack on Russia began, which Hitler had always had in mind. S.S. commissioners visited various places, Auschwitz among them. At first they expressed doubts about that particular area on the grounds of its remoteness and the unhealthy, marshy surroundings. But one man saw these as positive advantages.

This was Rudolf Höss, a devout Roman Catholic and an equally devout worshipper of the Führer, who did most to build up Auschwitz in its early stages. Himmler had picked him out early on as a perfect concentration camp administrator and put him in charge of Dachau. Later he transferred to Sachsenhausen. In 1940 he strongly recommended Auschwitz largely because of its isolation. It nevertheless had a useful, well-established rail connection. Höss was to serve as its commandant from its foundation until 1943.

Slaughter of captured Russians began in October 1941. Soviet prisoners were delivered to the primitive camp and set to work extending it. At the same time some of them worked as slave labour constructing an I. G. Farben plant nearby. A number were also used as guinea-pigs for early experiments in gassing. Bullets in the back of the neck were an expensive way of killing people, and took a long time when the numbers were large. An economical disposal method was needed which would deal with many people at one go. The first tests were carried out with ordinary vehicle exhaust fumes fed into barns or closed trucks. Then came experiments with Zyklon B, prussic acid crystals which gave off lethal gas the moment they were exposed to air.

This technique was an immediate success: 600 prisoners of war and 250 from the camp hospital were efficiently eliminated.

In the summer of 1941 Himmler had told Höss that the 'final solution' of the Jewish question must be achieved as soon as possible. The Führer himself insisted on an all-out extermination programme. Smaller camps already established in Poland for liquidating members of inferior races – at Belzec, Majdanek, Treblinka and Sobibor – could not handle the numbers involved. Höss nevertheless dutifully visited Treblinka to study their murder methods. In the course of six months Treblinka had disposed of 80,000 prisoners, most of them Jews from the Warsaw ghetto, by carbon monoxide poisoning. This was nowhere near efficient enough.

With the encouragement of his superior, Adolf Eichmann, Höss decided on the use of Zyklon B. Its manufacturers, Degesch, or *Deutsche Gesellschaft zur Schädlingsbekampfung* (German Company for Pest Control), were eager to assure the S.S. of their ability to provide regular adequate supplies via their main distributors, Tesch and Stabenow.

Eichmann visited Auschwitz to discuss the whole process. The rounding up of Polish Jews must be completed and then followed by mass importation of Jews from other occupied countries. The camp must be organized down to the last little detail to guarantee a steady inflow and annihilation. There must be no blockages at any stage. The two men set themselves a task which even in its first phase would involve over a million people. It was a matter of logistics: that was how Höss viewed it right to the end, even while writing his memoirs as he awaited trial after the war, and during the trial itself. He was to state with pedantic pride that 'an improvement we made over Treblinka was that we built our gas chambers to accommodate 2,000 people at one time'. The same was true of Eichmann. Tracked down and brought to trial in Israel, he continued to justify his mathematics and their application, and was puzzled by any mention of moral issues.

Until the purpose-built gas chambers were completed, gassing was carried on in farmhouses which had been evacuated at the start of the area's development. At first the intake was comparatively small, but as the rate of transports increased, the strain on the camp's killing resources intensified. First there were all these men, women and children to be slaughtered. Then their corpses had to be disposed of. For a time they were buried in pits, but that took up too much space and the bodies began to stink and spread disease as they rotted. For reasons of space and sanitation the remains had to be reduced to ash. The first crematorium soon proved insufficient for the numbers going through daily. Up to 2,000 corpses at a time were burnt on wood pyres, and more were burnt on top of the mouldering bodies dumped in the pits from earlier killings. Vaster than medieval plague burials, these mass graves contained over 100,000 corpses by the end of November 1942.

Within a few months four crematoria were fully operational in Birkenau, two huge buildings and two smaller ones. The larger two had underground gas chambers into which victims went down a flight of steps, the sick and helpless being tossed down a concrete chute. The smaller buildings had their gas chambers on ground level. Three bodies at a time could be fed through each of 100 doors in the largest ovens. Working round the clock, the four units together could dispose of about 18,000 bodies every twenty-four hours, while the open pits coped with a further 8,000 in the same period.

At first little distinction was made between treatment of Jews and non-Jewish enemies of the Reich; criminals, political prisoners and members of 'inferior' nationalities stood an equal chance of being gassed. After the middle of 1943 the gas chambers were reserved for Jews and gipsies, while Aryans died by hanging, shooting, or phenol injections.

Selections within the camp were made from sick prisoners, those too weak for slave labour, or sometimes simply in order to empty a block and restock it with a new intake. Most prisoners had to pass a selection the moment they arrived. Mother and I, and others in our group from Dresden, had escaped this because we were political prisoners. For most, that selection on the station ramp was their first encounter with Auschwitz methods; for many it was their last.

Dazed after long journeys, perhaps resigned to the prospect of hard labour in a foreign land, but rarely dreaming of imminent death, new-comers would tumble out of stinking trucks on to the ramp. Until June 1944 this was concealed from the rest of the camp, but when the railway extensions were completed it stood right by the entrance to Birkenau's extermination buildings. Transports came from all over Europe, some of them made up of sixty to eighty trucks at a time, carrying up to 20,000 people daily. Poles evacuated from their home regions because these were needed for German colonists heard they were to be resettled elsewhere; and were then delivered to Auschwitz. Jews from other lands were told the same lies. Some countries co-operated readily. Slovakia, which had taken advantage of Hitler's invasion of Czecho-slovakia to break loose from the Czechs and declare itself independent (a dubious independence, under Hitler's wing), willingly rounded up Jews and was pressured into paying 500 marks for each one removed and also to cover transportation costs.

Many Jews were encouraged before leaving to take money, gold and treasured possessions with them to provide for life in their new settlements. As soon as they reached Auschwitz their luggage was taken from them and piled high on the station ramp. They were assured these belongings could be reclaimed once they had been through the decontamination process. But the owners were barely off the ramp before special work parties began removing and sorting the goods.

On that ramp stood an S.S. doctor. As the columns of new arrivals moved towards him he would make a snap decision on the physical fitness of the younger men and women. Those he considered fit for work were waved to the left and dealt with much as my mother and I had been dealt with on arrival. The unfit, and all older people and children, were waved to the right. Any fears were soothed by promises that they were being sent to a camp where they would be well looked after, and where those unfit for work could take care of the children. In fact they were heading straight for the crematorium gates.

No Jewish child was allowed to live, and no Jewish mothers could produce children. Even a younger woman capable of work would be sent for immediate gassing if she was known to be pregnant. Over 1,000 Polish Jewish children, who had been temporarily lodged and well fed in the showpiece ghetto of Terezín (Theresienstadt) in Czechoslovakia, were told by the S.S. that they were to be exchanged with children from abroad. Parents and friends saw them off in high spirits, but never set eyes on them again. Every one went to Auschwitz and straight into the gas chambers.

The S.S. smiled and spoke reassuringly to new arrivals for as long as possible. What appeared to be a Red Cross van following the right-hand group as it moved off made stories about a camp for the sick and elderly all the more plausible. A crowd lulled into a sense of security was easier to handle than one broken up by hysteria. Only if someone grew argumentative did the true face of the guards show. Then they would kick the complainant back into line or turn their dogs loose to tear at the victim's flesh; or, if things really got out of hand, they would take the offender behind the nearest building and put a bullet into the nape of his or her neck.

Inside the gates another S.S. detail took over. Translators would tell the newcomers that they must now go through a disinfection chamber. It wouldn't take long. In the first room they would find rows of numbered coat-hooks. 'Please make a note of your numbers so there'll be no muddle when you come back from the showers.'

Obediently they undressed and went naked through doors at the far end of the room. The moment those doors had been locked, the deceptive Red Cross van drew up outside, usually carrying the S.S. doctor who had been present at the selection on the ramp. Two S.S. men got out and put gas masks on. They hurried up the slope above the underground gas chamber, or climbed a ladder to the roof if working on one of the smaller ones, and lifted flaps above the vent. In dropped the Zyklon B crystals, and they beat a hasty retreat. Twenty minutes to half an hour later, ventilators were switched on to disperse the gas.

With the doors open again, members of the *Sonderkommando* or Special Squad went in. Clothes and shoes were brought out from the changing room, ready for fumigation and despatch to distribution points all over Germany. If any of the recipients of such clothing suspected its origin, they kept quiet about it. Jewish dentists allocated to the *Kommando* went in among the corpses and removed gold teeth or gold fillings. Then the *Sonderkommando* hauled out the corpses, some of whom might well have been their own relatives, and carted them into the crematorium, where other members of the squad shovelled them into the furnaces.

Only occasionally was there any show of rebellion on an incoming transport. One of the most remarkable cases was that of a young woman so attractive that the S.S. officer in charge that day, a man called Schillinger, relaxed his guard and came close for a better look. She grabbed his revolver, shot him dead, and shot the man beside him through the leg. Her end was violent, but at least it was mercifully swift.

Few people nowadays appreciate the vastness of Auschwitz at its operational peak. I didn't fully grasp it myself until I returned in 1978, since no inmate was ever allowed to wander about freely between the different sections or ask questions. Even in 1978 it was hard to take in its size; little remained of the original industrial complex, but from what I had read in the intervening years and what I now pieced together I could conjure up a broad picture.

With forty sub-camps and purpose-built factory compounds, it in fact covered some twenty-five square miles. The original camp of Auschwitz I was occupied by the central administration for the whole concern, Gestapo H.Q., accommodation for representatives of various armament and other firms with military contracts, and political prisoners of all nationalities. Officers and S.S. garrison were housed there, along with the torture bunkers and medical experimentation block. Auschwitz II, or Birkenau, was primarily an extermination centre, but until your hour of death came you slaved for the glory of the Reich. Auschwitz III provided labour for building, and later operating, huge synthetic chemical and fuel works at Monowice, and controlled subsidiary camps dealing with agriculture, fish farming and coal mines. Krupp, Siemens and other well-known combines set up their factories in the neighbourhood.

The I. G. Farben concern, for which I had already worked in Bitterfeld, was among the first to establish a plant in the locality, producing ersatz rubber and fuels needed by Hitler's war machine. Before investing in the venture the company made a condition that cheap labour should be provided from the pool of prisoners in the concentration camp, both for plant construction and for productive work. The S.S. undertook to deliver the required number of prisoners at a daily rate of 6 marks per man, and also undertook to replace exhausted prisoners without delay. These employees were literally worked to death. If a prisoner was too feeble to make even a pretence of continuing at his job, he might be beaten to death on the factory floor; if he somehow made it back to the camp, he would surely be on the next selection for the gas chambers.

Directors of this and other factories protested more than once to the camp commandant about the inadequacy of the slave workers. Few could do a full day's work effectively on the rations provided, and few lived long enough to get the hang of a specialized job. Even when a skilled craftsman happened to be among the work force provided, there was no guarantee that he would be allowed to live any longer than the rest. Complaints were passed higher up, and the answer was swift: the directors should mind their own business. Although they were entitled to draw from this vast labour pool and pay for prisoners' services at a ridiculously low rate, the main purpose of Auschwitz was still to demoralize its inmates and ultimately kill them off.

Auschwitz nevertheless continued to be a profit-making enterprise almost until the end. The accumulation of possessions brought in by hundreds of thousands of prisoners made it the biggest black market in Europe. No matter how much their senior executives might complain, the factories achieved an output which might have been higher with healthy employees but still could hardly lose money when paying only a pittance to the half-dead. The S.S. got the biggest rake-off. They estimated the cost of keeping one prisoner in the camp at less than one-tenth of the average rate they charged the firms. And when the remains of human beings were despatched to the gas chambers and the crematoria, soap was made of fats drained from the bodies, fertilizer from bones, and cloth and felt from human hair.

And, of course, human beings were used in the laboratories. Experiments were carried out on living human flesh as culture for producing bacteria. Surgical operations were performed by S.S. doctors without anaesthetics in order to observe the full effects on the patient. In Block 10, women prisoners were subjected to painful tests designed to sterilize thousands of women in the most economic way, ensuring that Jews and Slavs and others could be rendered incapable of reproduction. These guinea-pigs were exposed to blistering X-rays for minutes on end. Sexual organs were hacked about. Poisonous injections were made direct into the womb, after which ovaries were removed and sent for examination in Berlin and other medical centres. In Auschwitz, not all members of the medical profession felt it their duty to assuage human suffering. Then, as now, many were keener on research and making a name in scientific circles than on alleviating pain. Many S.S. doctors held high positions in civilian hospitals in the Reich. Some were professors at university teaching hospitals, given permission to conduct experiments in Auschwitz in their special fields. One was actually the Chairman of the German Red Cross. The coldest and most calculating of them all was Dr Mengele.

He was a tall, good-looking man with blank eyes which made you feel he cared for nothing. Yet he did care. He was fascinated by twins, and if any came into the camp he would set them aside for his personal attention. They would be examined together and separately, and Mengele would have one killed to study the effect on the other. If any abnormality was discovered in one during a post-mortem, he would personally shoot the other and open the corpse to make a comparison.

Mengele's mistress was Irma Grese, a heavy but very beautiful blonde girl, only twenty when she entered Auschwitz. Soon she was put in charge of more than 30,000 women. She gloated over the use of her bullhide whip and walking stick, and sometimes carried a rubber truncheon with which to batter prisoners senseless. Among her other favourite activities was gardening. She had a well-kept kitchen garden within the camp, trimly surrounded by neat white stones. In post-war newspapers and at her trial she was better known for her infamies at Belsen; but she and Kramer, the 'Beast of Belsen', had learnt their trade and done far more damage at Auschwitz. She took particular pleasure in standing beside Mengele to make selections from the women: some for experimentation, some for immediate death.

Mengele was captured by the Allies at the end of the war. He feigned illness, escaped from hospital, and finished up in South America. All attempts to extradite him failed; attempts to capture him, as Eichmann was so daringly captured, failed. S.S. money helped him to get away and kept him in comfort far from the scene of his crimes. The S.S. money runs into millions. It came from the sale of valuables taken from prisoners on incoming transports. Proceeds of these robberies were banked on behalf of the S.S. in Swiss banks, and used after the war to fund refugees from the vengeance of the victors. Much of it probably still lies there in Switzerland, untouchable.

As I mentioned earlier, the camp hierarchy was by no means made up entirely of German S.S. Its constitution and operation took some understanding, and the majority of inmates did not live long enough to learn it. One thing which was especially confusing was the power struggle between two elements in the camp. It was more marked, I think, in the men's than in the women's section; but the basic clash was the same. It arose between political prisoners and the criminal category of prisoners who in effect ruled the everyday life – and death – of their less favoured fellows.

When Auschwitz was created, the S.S. installed a number of professional criminals to handle camp organization and discipline. They were men and women who had been convicted of murder, rape, prostitution and robbery, and had lived in a criminal atmosphere most of their lives. But they were Germans, and in spite of any monstrosity they might have committed, this made them automatically superior to Jews, Slavs, or any other race. They made up the camp police and supervised lesser prisoners at work and in the blocks. Their leader, the *Lagerälteste*, was simply a highly qualified gang boss spreading terror in whatever way he or she chose, answerable only to the *Lagerführer*, the S.S. officer in charge of camp discipline, who in turn was answerable to the *Lagerkommandant* . . . who was answerable only to Berlin.

These criminals of German blood did not go through a quarantine period. They were assigned to *Kapo* duties straightaway, with a chance of speedy promotion if they behaved well enough – that is, badly enough. Below them in hierarchy were Poles, Esthonians, Hungarians and others who spoke good German and were ready to adopt German ways. But the proudest boast any prisoner could make was that he or she was a Reich German – killer, prostitute, drug peddler or not.

The real struggle for domination of the camp's internal machinery was between these criminals and the increasing number of political detainees. The political group included, for example, men and women Communists who had been rounded up long ago and had passed through a succession of concentration camps. Many had acquired general respect for their staying power. Ultimately they were the only ones with any chance of standing up against the criminals, for most of them, too, were Reich Germans, but with better education and higher standards.

During my spell in Auschwitz the political element battled its way to the fore. In Birkenau, after a campaign of which we got only the most puzzling echoes, we found ourselves with a *Lagerälteste* named Orli who had suffered years of imprisonment as a political dissident. Conditions improved during our time with her. There was still brutality, because that was part of official policy; but she did succeed in making things less awful than they had been under the reign of the practised criminals.

In a gruesome way it was almost in the prisoners' interest to keep the camp functioning. If the administration collapsed, we could not fend for ourselves. If there had been a mass rebellion and a breakout, there was nowhere we could have gone. This was an inhospitable fringe of the country with little to live on and no one who would offer help. Refugees could soon be hunted down, if they didn't starve in the meantime. You could despair, or you could resolve to go along with the system: work up through the ranks of privileged prisoners and then turn on your one-time friends and treat them just as the S.S.-inspired bullies treated them. Mother would never play this foul game; neither would I. Yet we survived.

Even when the Nazis knew the war was lost they did not turn the inmates loose or slacken their persecution. Just the opposite. The extermination programme was stepped up and took priority over national defence. Badly needed trains were used to transport Jewish victims instead of transporting troops and arms to the front line. S.S. officers threw themselves with new zest into beating and murdering Jews rather than rush off to defend their Fatherland against the Russians, British and Americans. Only at the last moment did the authorities decide to evacuate Auschwitz and attempt to destroy the evidence of what they had been up to. Still they did not liberate the prisoners, but drove them out on transports and death marches as if to make sure that everyone would perish in the end, and suffer while waiting for the end.

I was not to know in 1943 that I would survive to see all this for myself. But something inside kept telling me that I had to last out. Never obey. Never give in. Some of us had to live, to defy them all, and one day tell the truth.

7

Organize or Die

KEEPING TRACK of time was impossible. One hour of the morning was memorable: four o'clock, when whistles screeched and there was shouting and bullying and you turned out for roll-call. But you soon lost track of the days and months. The seasons ran into one another. Summers could be hot and oppressive, with mosquitoes rising from the marshes and the mud baked hard. Between winter and summer it was difficult to tell quite where you were or what season came next. There was no way of working things out from the vegetation – there was not a blade of grass, only vast tracts of mud.

In winter the mud in the camp was deep and wet until, for a short period, it froze hard. At the wettest times the S.S. and their criminal subordinates took pleasure in ferreting out some minor infringement of the rules so that they could sentence an entire block to kneel in the mud for hours on end. This was known as *Sport*. When they were in a particularly savage mood they would order us to hold our arms above our heads. Anyone whose arms sagged was beaten up. Some sank into the mud and suffocated. Others were trampled into it.

Winter could be fatal unless you organized extra clothing. The one garment which you had been issued with, and never dared take off, gave little protection against the biting cold. Once, when on outside work, I managed to stuff paper from cement bags under my dress, wrapping it round my body as makeshift insulation.

It was little better indoors. There was rarely any fuel for the stove and heating channel. In a block which housed élite prisoners, many things were allowed, including wood for warming up the place; for the lower grades, nothing. Not only did you not get an issue of fuel, you were forbidden to organize it on your own, and unless you had a

Blockälteste who would close her eyes to a breach of regulations you could be in trouble. The only way you might get her to keep quiet was by smuggling wood in from outside rather than by breaking up planking from the bunks, which would mean trouble for her too if an S.S. inspection uncovered such a crime.

One night, desperate from the cold, I ventured out after curfew. Our *Blockälteste* at the time was Fat Berta, a buxom Hungarian woman with a big red face. She had grown plump on rations appropriated from those she was supposed to distribute to prisoners. Her favourite occupation was thumping and whipping girls about the head. But tonight she was sound asleep in her cosy little cubbyhole at the end of the block. My only problem was the *Torwache*, a prisoner deputed to stay awake and keep watch on the door to make sure nobody sneaked out after curfew. Not too much of a problem: tonight the *Torwache* was my mother.

What she was doing on my block at that time, I truly cannot recall. She served in the hospital compound almost her entire time in Auschwitz. But nothing was ever settled or reliable in that lunatic maze. In thirty days you could work in ten to fifteen different jobs, with perhaps no more than a couple of days in the same place. I find it well-nigh impossible to recollect things in proper sequence. One day you'd be on the hospital staff; the next, grabbed for work out of doors. I remember that for a brief period my mother was employed in the weaving shed, and during that period caught glimpses of my old boyfriend, Simon. Even privileged prisoners were never entirely secure: they could be thrown out of a job on the whim of a superior and then crawl their way back into another. You could be promoted, demoted, shifted sideways, left to your own devices or harassed to death.

What I do know is that my mother was on duty that night. I coaxed her into letting me out while Fat Berta was still snoring.

Earlier in the day I had noticed a large pile of wood at the back of the lavatories. I longed to get an armful and warm the stove briefly. If any of the girls had smuggled a few potatoes in, perhaps I'd be given a slice after we had heated them up. I got safely to the wood-pile and loaded myself with as many pieces as I could carry. But it wasn't as easy to crawl back as it had been to get out. Tottering across the space between one block and another, I was picked out by the sudden sweep of a searchlight. Somebody began to shout. I dropped the wood and ran.

It had been a bad night to choose. The S.S. usually left the camp and went off to their quarters after curfew, but on this occasion a few had for some reason stayed behind. One of the worst of them spotted me and began to chase me. It was Bohrmann, a scrawny woman with the sharp features of a weasel. I dashed into the block and flung myself under one of the *koje*. Bohrmann was close on my heels. She saw which block I had run into. Her screams of rage brought Fat Berta out. Faint, dismal light cast awful shadows along the floor.

'Everybody off! Come on, off your bunks!' Bohrmann was panting. 'Who was it who just ran in here?' When there was no reply she howled: 'Very well, then. If someone doesn't speak up there'll be a selection tomorrow. And those who are left will do *Sport*. And then the whole lot of you will be transferred to the S.K.' (The *Strafkompani* was the punishment squad from which no one ever returned alive.)

I crawled out and stood up. Bohrmann scurried up to me and slapped me across the face. Then she turned away to growl at Fat Berta. The girls nearest at once set on me, kicking and clawing, cursing me for having been caught and putting them in danger.

'Quiet!' Bohrmann had left, Berta was standing up on the heating channel and swinging her whip. 'Quiet, you bloody swine.' Then she jumped down and started swearing at my mother for having let me get out. Mother got the biggest beating she'd ever had. She could well have been killed if the other girls hadn't run to her rescue and begged the *Blockälteste* to leave her alone. Then they all turned on me again, until Berta grabbed my arm and dragged me off to her own cubicle, where she set about me on her own account. When she had finished, she breathed: 'Tomorrow at *Zählappell* you're going to be for it. Bohrmann's coming to fetch you.'

It was my second death sentence. This time I couldn't see any hope of a reprieve.

There was nowhere for me to sleep. Nobody would let me share their *koje*. I lay on the ground, awake all night. Even on a bunk I doubt if I could have slept.

At last the whistles blew for *Zählappell*. When the usual commotion was over, I had found myself a place right at the back. We stood in the cold, as usual, for two hours. Or maybe it was more. I was in no hurry for it to be ended: not this time.

But it had to end. The usual S.S. were there, and this time I spied some extras. Bohrmann was there, and beside her was *Rapportführer* Taube. It was no longer funny to think of calling him *Abortführer* behind his back. Whenever he entered the camp we sensed that something awful was going to happen; he had never been anything but a messenger of death. We were not supposed to look at people of his exalted rank. Always we had to stand at attention with our eyes down when such members of the master race came to inspect us. But we had all, at one time and another, sneaked glances. We knew Taube, with his deep-set, murderous little eyes, as bright in that slimy skin as the eyes of a snake. Now he was here in front of our block, waiting.

The *Lagerkapo* called out my number: 39934. I stepped forward. At once I was marched off, kicked and hit across the back of the head. I had no idea where they were taking me. Then we came to an enclosed area which I realized was a section of the S.K. punishment compound. It didn't need those fences to keep people out: nobody ever wanted to stray near it. As we got closer I heard screams. Someone was lying face down in the mud being flogged.

I felt a crazy sense of relief. If I was being brought here, then I was not going to be put to death at once. All last night I had been expecting a trip to the gas chambers. Maybe it was only going to be a flogging.

I was right.

'You're to have twenty-five strokes,' Bohrmann announced. 'And get them right, because every time you make a mistake we go back to the beginning and start again.'

At least the spiteful little Bohrmann was small and wiry, and wouldn't have all that much strength for whipping. Then I saw Taube rolling up his sleeves. This must be the end. I was grabbed from behind, and two *Kapos* thrust me down on a low trestle.

'Get ready to count. Remember – miscount, and the strokes start all over again.'

The whip had twenty-five separate strands, so that one blow was in effect twenty-five lashes anyway.

I couldn't believe the pain of it. The first lash; I called out 'One'. The second was worse, and I called out again. The blows fell all over me, some on my buttocks, some slicing into my legs. One or two were over my head and into my neck. I remember counting up to six, and I think somehow I must have managed seven or eight. After that I remember nothing – until the whistles started blowing.

It must be *Zählappell* time. I tried to move my head. *Zählappell* . . . I had to go, there'd be trouble if I wasn't there . . . must go . . . But I couldn't lift my head. When I tried to move my arm I felt something wet, but I was too numb to find out what it was. My body was all wet underneath. Must be the mud. And I felt something sticky on my thigh. When I tried to ease one hand towards it I found a hole there. How could I be so wet when it wasn't raining?

I forced my eyes open. I was lying in the mud, but that wasn't where the wetness was coming from. I was soaked in blood. Then there were voices. None of them meant anything. I couldn't be bothered with them. An awful throbbing pain built up until there wasn't an inch of me free from it.

'This lot – waiting for the lorries.' A *Kapo* was plodding her way between heaps of bodies. 'Come on, shift them.' Out of the corner of my eye I saw her kick one or two. 'Right, that's dead. Not sure about this one.'

'Better go on the heap?'

'No. Just a minute.' A foot in my hip turned me half over. 'Look, she's still alive. Must be for Block 25.'

'No,' I tried to protest, 'I don't go to Block 25. I belong . . . I have to get back . . . Block number . . .'

'You're in the penal company, you don't go anywhere.'

There was a commotion. It must be *Zählappell*. People were rushing to and fro, dropping whatever job they were on in order to get back to their blocks. I grabbed someone and whimpered. 'Take me to . . .'

But I couldn't stand, and they were in a hurry, and although a couple of women tried to help me they couldn't make out what on earth I was trying to say.

Yet somehow there I was, back at the edge of our block. And my mother. What was she doing here? I learned dazedly that she had been desperately trying to find out my fate, and had been beaten up by a *Kapo* while wandering about looking for me. Now she hauled me inside the block.

'But you're not supposed to be back here, after being sent to the S.K. What are you going to do during *Zählappell*?'

Whatever happened, I mustn't be on roll-call. Not in any position where I'd be seen, anyway. Fat Berta might not know every face on the block, but after last night's uproar she would remember mine. I asked if anyone had died that day. Girls scurrying in and out assured us that a lot had died. A whole batch had been carried off on a cart.

'I'll stay on, then,' I said. 'I'll hide right at the back of the group.'

There was a gaping open wound on my thigh, bleeding badly. One of my eyes was completely closed. I couldn't tell why, or what it looked like to anyone else, since there was no such thing as a mirror here. But in the commotion and the roll-call I thought I could get by, provided there was no close inspection. Mother left me, and I braced myself for the ordeal.

I was half dead, but then so were a lot of others. No face-by-face inspection was carried out along the back rank, and Bohrmann didn't bother to come looking for me. Maybe she assumed I had been thrown aside as dead and swept up in the regular corpse collection. And by now she would surely have found another victim, anyway.

It was essential to remain concealed. Above all, to avoid Berta's notice. I managed to get myself cleaned up, and kept out of the way until there was a chance of getting across to the hospital compound. There was no question of my being admitted for treatment. Wounds received during punishment did not merit medical attention. But I pretended I had a fever. It was not difficult. I could hardly walk straight, and was still in such pain that I could hardly speak coherently. A young woman I had seen once before, and who knew and respected my mother, got me in and on to a bunk. I had two days' rest before a less friendly assistant realized I had no business being there and hustled me out before there was trouble.

They were hunting for work parties that day, and I allowed myself to be caught so that I could try to insinuate myself into another block.

It was still winter when my new *Blockälteste* informed us we were all to attend a delousing and disinfection session. I was overjoyed. The colonies of lice which had settled on my body had been steadily growing. I had tried to cover the holes left by oozing pus with paper, but when I pulled it away it often made a larger hole. I am still pitted with the marks from those days. And there were fleas, always swarming under your garment. Shake it, and they fell out by the score.

Privileged prisoners could get into the sauna for private sessions. You could always spot them by their smarter, brighter look and their longer hair. If you had long hair it indicated that you had escaped the mass delousings and shavings, just as wearing leather boots instead of clogs showed you were a skilful organizer, someone who knew the ropes and ought to be treated with respect.

I hadn't acquired that status, so for me it was mass disinfection along with women from other blocks. Thousands of us went into the sauna naked, dumping our clothes. As well as the S.S. women, a number of S.S. men stood sniggering and idly flicking their whips. They kept well back, though. The S.S. were scared of contracting typhus. On one occasion a prisoner deliberately scraped a handful of lice from her body and flung them in the face of a guard who had come too close. She died immediately; but after that the S.S. were even more careful to keep their distance.

'Legs and arms out! Right out!' Girls inside the sauna quickly shaved our pubic hair, armpits and head.

Beside enormous drums of blue fluid were women with large mops. They smeared the oily mess over our bodies and heads. Then we stampeded on to the showers, fighting for precious seconds under the trickles of lukewarm water. You were lucky to get even slightly wet. There was certainly not enough water to wash all that evil fluid off your skin; and of course there was no soap and not a towel in sight. After a few minutes the showers were turned off.

At the end of the session we ought to have been able to reclaim our clothes, which had been taken away to be cleaned, or even get a clean new set. But on this occasion there were no new clothes. There was no question of a shortage, but for some reason none were available for us. While we milled about, teeth chattering, clinging to one another to share what little warmth we could muster, the familiar whistles began to sound.

'*Zählappell. Zählappell. Alles anstellen.*'

We couldn't believe we would be expected to line up naked in this terrible cold for the usual evening roll-call. But there was no way of escaping that holy ritual. Without a stitch of clothing we were bullied into rows of five. The only women wearing anything were the *Blockälteste* and her assistants.

A bitter sleeting rain began. By the end of two hours there were scores of women on the ground. Some died of exposure. I couldn't feel anything any more. I kept telling myself this was a good thing: if I couldn't even feel the cold, either I was in good health or I was ready for death. It didn't matter. My body was numb. And my soul? Well, that part of me had been dead a long time now.

At last we were allowed back inside our block. I would have to summon up the strength to climb on to the mattress, under the blanket. But there was no mattress, no blanket. Our bunks were completely bare. Everything had been taken away for delousing. We had to settle down naked on the wood, huddling together. There was fighting all through the night, for everybody wanted to be on the inside of the bunks to keep warm. *Zählappell* in the morning was just the same. We stood and froze; or collapsed and died.

It was late afternoon when at last there was a shout that clothes had come. Whole cartloads had arrived, in fact, but instead of being issued to us they had simply been thrown on the roof of the block to dry. As it was still raining, they stayed wet. Not until the third day did the *Blockälteste* decide to send her assistants up a ladder to start throwing the garments down. They were still soaking wet, but we longed for them, grabbing whatever we could. There was plenty to choose from, because so many inmates had died during these last few days. I even managed to get hold of a pair of shoes – real leather shoes after all that time in clogs!

Many of the girls who had just managed to survive our three-day ordeal were so ill that they had to be taken into the hospital. So few remained in our block that we were redistributed among other blocks; so once more I found myself in a new place.

This time I had been lucky. I was transferred to a compound of

Funktion Häftlinge – prisoners with better jobs. Some worked in the kitchens, the clothing stores, or in the sauna. And some, like me, were no more than cunning dodgers. With my passable clothes and leather shoes, I looked so important that the block staff were not sure what to make of me and so left me well alone.

It was about now that I was reunited with Hanka and Genia, the two sisters who had come with us from Dresden. Genia worked in the sauna and was able to smuggle in friends for a decent wash, one at a time. Such luxury! She even got a change of clothes for us. Once, too, she wangled me into a concert given for the S.S. and privileged prisoners in the sauna. The camp orchestra played under the baton of Alma Rosé, daughter of the former first violinist in a symphony orchestra, and the niece of Gustav Mahler. It was grotesque.

Lesser prisoners were sometimes given orchestral performances, but not in the best of circumstances. It was quite common for the musicians to play in front of them while they were undergoing *Sport*, on their knees with their arms above their heads. But occasionally they had a treat. To make up a full audience, a number of prisoners would be rounded up and ordered to attend, maybe along with some of the sick from the hospital. S.S. officers and privileged prisoners in the front rows might turn and nod condescendingly, especially if they applauded at the right places; and the very next day might send the same people to the gas chamber.

Alma Rosé was not particularly attractive, but she was a gifted violinist. She probably thought that she and her celebrated father were safe from the Nazis, being at the top of their profession. But while performing in Holland she was seized and sent to the camp without being able to get in touch with her father or anyone back home in Germany. She made up to the authorities in order to keep her privileges, and above all so that she might continue living for music, no matter how inadequately played on the odd selection of instruments which made up the orchestra.

Our own impromptu concerts were much more relaxed. In the evenings we sang and recited poetry, and on one occasion devised a complete ballet within the confines of our hut. Such things were only possible when you had a fairly tolerant *Blockälteste*. Hanka, Genia and I used to get together and dream up different backgrounds for our lives. Nothing too ambitious: we just pretended we were on a better block, with a few tiny luxuries. But then Hanka would begin to peer longingly into a more distant future. Standing on the heating channel she would dance and wave her arms, telling us again what she had told us in that prison cell so long ago: 'When we get out of here I'm going to be an actress.' We all clapped and cheered. Even the *Blockälteste* used to come out and laugh.

Such gaiety didn't last. We would grow more serious and talk of what we'd do to *Them* – our tormentors – when we got out. If we got out. And how much we'd appreciate the silly little everyday things which ordinary people take for granted. How happy we would feel just to be free, to sit in a chair or lie in bed, to have food and water, even just to be allowed to saunter about in a street. Yes, if ever we were free again we would always stay happy and smiling.

One thing I needed very much: regular visits to my mother. She was back working in the hospital compound, but I couldn't just walk over and say good afternoon. I had to take advantage of the usual commotion after morning roll-call and smuggle myself into the *Revier*, the hospital compound, which was not easy. Then at the end of the day there was the business of getting back to my block during the commotion before evening roll-call. Every time I did this I was risking my life. You learned to take such risks all the time.

I also contrived a succession of visits to the dentist in order to snatch a few moments close to Mother. To justify these sessions I had to have something done to my teeth. Claiming a raging toothache, I would ask for holes to be drilled or quite tiny cavities enlarged. There were no such things as fillings so I had to think up all kinds of ingenious excuses. Once or twice I asked for a gaping hole to be drilled right through a tooth, and then later claimed it was hurting so much that I had to go back and have it seen to. The dentist was himself a prisoner and played along; but we had to be wary of the S.S. woman on duty.

A fully operational dental surgery in an extermination camp was as crazy as the existence of the hospital. Prisoners who were ill, most of them with typhus, would be taken into hospital for treatment and stay there recuperating for a few weeks. Then, without warning, the wards would be completely emptied to make room for more patients, while the previous occupants were shunted immediately into the gas chambers. One day the camp commandant would order that ailing prisoners should be allowed out for a spell in the sunshine. Next day there would be a special roll-call at which many of them would be selected for death.

The contradictions were deliberately engineered to bewilder you so hopelessly that you gave in. Total obedience, total humiliation. It was no use trying to predict logically what they would do. Yet at the same time you had to be somehow a step ahead. You had to develop special antennae. There might be a rumour at curfew, or a glimpse of an S.S. 'angel of death' entering the camp at an unusual time would alert you to some punishment, or a selection. And if you suspected your own block was going to be picked on you might risk fleeing to another during the roll-call commotion. If your assessment was right you lived another day or week or month. If it was wrong you were as good as dead.

All the time you had to anticipate their illogicalities and be ready to dodge whatever trick they sprang. If there was apparent good news, there had to be something wicked behind it. Nothing was to be believed; nothing but the worst. Refuse inward submission. Above all keep away from those who said it wasn't worth trying to go on. Despair was contagious. Despair turned you into a *Muselmann.*

There was one period when illness had almost the same awful effect on me. It started with a night when I couldn't sleep, tired as I was. I tossed and turned, hot and shivery, icy cold and then bathed in sweat. Was it typhus? Nearly everyone caught it sooner or later. It was as common a killer as the S.S.

In the morning I tried to get up. My legs felt as if they were made of cotton wool. My knees bent under me and I collapsed. Immediately after morning roll-call I was dragged to the *Revier.* I remember begging the *Blockälteste* over and over again to see I was taken to Block 12. That was where my mother was working.

The block was full. I was put on to a single bunk which already had three occupants. One patient had diphtheria, another malaria, and the third had typhus. There was no doubt about it: I too had typhus.

Mother was a *Nachtwache*, a sort of night nurse whose main duty was to see that no one left the block during the hours of darkness. Desperately ill patients were continually trying to get out, imagining in their delirium that cars were waiting to take them home or that they had to catch a train. There were continuous screams and moans of '*Nacht-wache*, basin . . . *Nachtwache*, a drink . . . water . . .' I heard myself crying out for water. Then I must have been unconscious for a long time. Then awake, or half awake. I thought I could see oranges, grapes and cool drinks at the foot of my bunk and screamed for them. No one would pass them to me. Mother was there, and I cursed her for being so cruel. The pain in my head was excruciating, the thirst unbearable. Nothing to quench it, only dry bread, until my mother cooked some potato soup and tried to pour it down my throat. I lost count of time. It didn't matter. Nothing mattered. If I could have got up and walked I would not have wanted to.

One day as I lay unconscious there was a selection. All those unable to get up were taken to be gassed. Mother saw what would surely happen to me. She pushed me inside a straw mattress and laid a corpse on top of me, praying I would keep still and not start raving and singing, as I had been doing for some hours earlier. The S.S. doctor passed the bunk. The corpse was taken away. The incurably sick were taken also. I was still alive.

After days of unconsciousness I began slowly to grasp where I was and what was going on around me. I had first to learn to sit up, then gradually to walk. With each step my heart pounded. My legs were like matchsticks and only bones were visible. My body was covered with infected boils and scratches, and there was a rat bite on my forehead. None of it mattered. I was in danger of giving up and letting myself become a *Muselmann*.

Mother talked to me, though all she got in return was rambling nonsense. I did not even recognize her. But she persevered, slowly and steadily drawing me back to life.

When anyone was on the way to recovery she had to be sent back to the camp to work. It was not always possible to get back to one's own original block, and often those who had had good jobs before their illness found themselves condemned to *Aussenarbeit*. Mother begged her *Blockälteste* to let me remain in the hospital compound for the time being. The woman relented, and I stayed on.

During my convalescence another selection was carried out on Block 12. That day I was able to walk, but not very well. Mother was worried, too, about the sores and scratches on my body. And I was far too thin. One by one we had to parade naked outside. Mengele himself was there. He ordered us to run. Those who could not summon up the energy to run were sent to the left, the others to the right. I gathered all my strength, began to run, and somehow made it. But Mengele was staring hard at my pimply body. He made me turn round, then round again, while he hesitated . . . and at last pointed to the right.

I was still very weak, and standing naked for hours made me ill again. This time it looked like pneumonia. Mother sat by me night after night, again cooking soup and trying desperately to stop me scratching the *Krätze* which disfigured my whole body. My hair, which had grown two or three inches long since last being shaved, began to come out in handfuls until I was totally bald. Inflammations and abscesses developed in both my ears. Some days later a prisoner doctor pierced these with a knitting needle, which made me completely deaf for some weeks.

After three months in Block 12 my health just would not improve. I couldn't get the camp food down, kept on coughing, lost all will to live. The perfect *Muselmann*. The more my memory came back, the more I despaired. Now the *Blockälteste* was coming daily to warn that

I had been here far too long and must be on my way. Mother kept pleading with her. Eventually, as a great favour, it was agreed that I could be transferred to work in Block 29, the dysentery block.

At last I was on the staff. This meant various privileges and comforts. For one thing, you didn't have to go out for roll-call. Above all it meant you were less liable to be selected for the gas chamber.

My job was that of a *Putzerin*: camp jargon for a cleaner or orderly. After a while I was promoted to the rank of *Pflegerin*, a nurse. I distributed rations to the sick – most of whom were too far gone to be able to eat anyway – and every three or four days took water round. The rest of the time was spent carrying out the dead. This was no easy task, for I was still so weak that I could not lift a body. Most of them had to be tipped off the bunks and then dragged along the floor.

In the typhus block I had just left, my mother found herself looking after Alma Rosé, the orchestra leader. She nursed her through the usual delirium; and Alma, unlike many others, returned to her original post. But soon she was back in hospital again, in the strangest circumstances. Apparently she had been told she was to be released from Birkenau to entertain troops at the front. This she was not unwilling to do; in spite of everything she was in many ways more German than Jewish, and could even feel patriotic about the Nazi régime. Girls in her orchestra often suffered from the vagaries of this dual personality. Just before she was due to leave, some privileged prisoners arranged a farewell party. Halfway through it she was stricken with sudden illness and had to be rushed into hospital. A stomach pump was used, but too late: she was dead. Mother told me, and most people believed, that she must have been poisoned by a jealous woman prisoner who resented her release, but nothing was ever proved.

In her book *The Musicians of Auschwitz*, Fania Fénelon describes an incredible scene in which Alma Rosé's corpse was laid out in the infirmary and covered by the S.S. with masses of white flowers. Members of the S.S. filed past with tears in their eyes.

In Block 29, as in the typhus block, selections took place frequently. Sometimes two or three hundred patients were taken for gassing in one week. Usually the camp doctors, Mengele, Rohde or König, came to the hospital huts in person to make the selections. At other times Rohde would come to take blood samples for his own experiments. Although he was under Mengele's thumb, he actually tried to improve conditions in the hospital, and prisoner doctors working with him were able to persuade him to help other prisoners. But when it came to a selection, there was never any sign of pity. The doctor, flanked by what looked like a medical commission of privileged German prisoners, made everyone line up on one side of the heating channel. Those who were agile enough to jump over the channel might be spared. All those too ill to stand were lost from the start. Sometimes prisoner doctors were ordered to hand in the numbers of the seriously ill, and the S.S. doctor would walk from bunk to bunk chalking crosses on them and ticking off the numbers on his list. The numbers were of patients selected to be gassed.

Then came what I still remember as my worst day in Auschwitz. There are many things I have managed to put out of my mind, or at least to blur over as years have gone by; but this I shall never forget.

A couple of weeks previously my friends Hanka and Genia had both been admitted to my block. They were in a pretty bad state, but there was every sign that they would recover. I was so glad to look after them and be able to do things for them. Soon after they arrived there was a selection, but it was not carried out with the usual efficiency, and I managed to imitate my mother's methods and hide the two of them inside a bulky straw mattress.

Mother came to the block that dreadful day with a birthday present for me. How she had managed to keep track of the months and days I don't really know. 'Many happy returns of the day,' she said, and gave me an onion – a wonderful luxury. But soon after she had gone, green uniforms could be seen entering the *Revier*. Another selection. It was to be on our block. This time it was not only for the dying: the whole hut was to be cleared, and all except the staff were to die.

The doctor with *Lagerführerin* Haase, *Rapportführer* Taube and others made their way through the block poking into and under every bunk, driving the patients outside. Some convalescents tied themselves to their bunks, but it was no good. The S.S. made us untie them and drag them out along with the rest. There was no way of hiding Hanka and Genia this time, or anyone else.

I had hoped we might somehow get them on to a staff position when they were fit again. Keep them off external work, find them something indoors with a few little privileges and a few comforts. Now I had to help load them on to the lorries which waited to take them on their last journey. It was the same with the sick as with corpses: it took two of you, one at the shoulders and one at the legs, picking up the limp or struggling body, swinging it once, twice, to and fro, and then throwing it up on to the heap in the lorry.

We screamed and wept as we did it. And when I saw that Hanka was one of those I had to toss up in that way, I knew I would have to go with her. Instead of picking up another victim, I made a dash for the lorry and tried to scramble up behind my friends. Mother, who had been watching horror-stricken from the edge of the block, saw what I was doing. She ran across, and with a couple of friends on the staff dragged me away. The S.S. didn't seem to care one way or the other. I wished they would come and push mother out of the way and throw me up themselves. But they let us settle it between us. I was held back until the lorry had rumbled off. Then we staggered back into the empty block and collapsed on the floor, weeping.

Still I wanted to die. With my own hands I had helped to send two dear friends to their death. I could never forget the pleading, terrified look in their eyes.

Until then I had struggled to survive. Now there was no fight left in me. I ought to have gone on the lorry. But there was still the fence. 'Going on the fence' meant a wild dash across one of the trenches and then it would be all over in seconds. If you could get that close, the electricity in the fence actually drew you into it.

Mother would not take her eyes off me.

'Pull yourself together,' she said over and over again. 'We'll be out of here one day. We've *got* to live until we can get out. You'll see.' And, over and over again: 'You mustn't give up, not now. Mustn't give up.'

I repeated it to myself, but couldn't believe it. I didn't throw myself on the fence; but for days I walked aimlessly around not knowing what to do with myself. 'I must not give up, must not give up, must not give up.' It must have helped. There was hardly a spark of life left in me, but somehow it was just enough to keep me going after all.

8

The Riches of Kanada

WHILE THE staff on Block 29 were still numbed by the shock of that complete clearance, a *Lagerälteste* came to visit us.

'We're forming a new night shift for the *Effektenkommando*. If any of you want to join, you can do so.'

It was rare to be offered a choice of anything. Normally you did as you were told and took what jobs you were given.

This squad was a special one. We had all heard rumours about the luxuries you could grab for yourself if you worked in it: such an abundance of everything that in camp slang it was called the *Kanada Kommando* after that far-off country which for some reason was associated with all the riches the heart could desire.

The comforts organized by girls in this Effects Squad came from a mysterious sub-camp a couple of miles up the railway line. The girls would never breathe a word of what went on there, but when they returned to their block each evening you marvelled at how well dressed and well fed they looked. Also they were good at smuggling things in: warm clothes, shoes, food, and other treats to barter. No wonder they could afford to look so superior!

There was one snag. Girls working in the *Kanada Kommando* tended to disappear after a time without trace. Selections had that effect on many a block, but there was something even more disturbing than usual about the regularity with which this squad was obliterated and restocked with newcomers. Nobody in it was ever returned or transferred to any other duty.

Mother insisted I should take the opportunity. It would take me away from the hospital block with its dreadful memories, and good food would build me up again. And if there were so many goods of one kind and another to be smuggled back into the main camp, they could be used for our benefit and the benefit of other needy prisoners. I agreed to take the job.

Only when this was settled did we learn to our dismay that the routine was about to be altered. The new *Kanada II* would live in a compound beside their work and no longer make the daily journey to and fro. When I said goodbye to my mother that fine spring day in 1944 we didn't know if we would ever see each other again.

The orchestra played us out through the main gate. We turned left. For some time there was nothing to be seen on either side but camp fences and huts. At last we came to green fields, marvellous after the brown, sticky mud we were used to. Wild flowers were already blooming, and far away against the sky were the mountains – my very own mountains, above my home. We came to a beautiful little wood. It was only then that the meaning of the camp's name dawned on me. Birkenau in German, and Brzezinki in Polish, both mean the place of birch trees; and this wooded countryside was full of them.

On the far side of this small forest was the camp. The peculiar low, red brick buildings were each dominated by two very tall, wide, square chimneys. As we marched through the gate I recognized the outlines of a sauna on the left. Behind it was a well-cultivated plot of vegetables, and beyond that a white house surrounded by beautiful lawns and flower beds, giving the impression of a holiday resort.

Further inside the camp was a proper road, the main *Lagerstrasse*. To the right, a narrower road beside which stood two rows of well-built huts, six or seven to a row. Directly at the back of the huts were toilets and then a wire fence. Immediately behind the fence was one of the brick buildings with its two tall chimneys. Close by were three more. By the last hut on the left-hand side was a huge heap – it looked like a mountain – as high as a three-storey building. Goods of every description were jumbled up: suitcases, bundles of clothing, shoes, prams and even toys. Beyond the heap was another fence, dividing our camp from that of the men.

Our huts were luxurious in comparison with those we had left behind. There were only about 300 girls to a hut, and the three-tier single bunks had well-filled straw mattresses and two blankets each. There were even proper windows – they looked out on to those ominous buildings.

We had scarcely been inside a few minutes when Isa, a girl I had chatted to on the way here, pulled me to the window.

'You must see this. Look!'

I didn't want to look. I was too afraid of what I might see. But I had to go and stand beside her. Not fifty yards away was an incredible sight. A column of people had been shuffling from the direction of the railway line into a long, low hall. When the place was full there was a delay; but I went on watching, hypnotized. What I was witnessing was murder, not of one person, but of hundreds of innocent people at a time. Of course we had known, had whispered about it, and been terrified of it from a distance; but now I was *seeing* it, right there in front of me.

On the outside of the low building a ladder had been placed. A figure in S.S. uniform climbed briskly up. At the top he pulled on a gas mask and gloves, tipped what looked from here like a white powder into an opening in the roof, and then hurried back down the ladder and ran off. Screams began to come out of the building. We could hear them echoing across to our hut, the desperate cries of suffocating people. I held my breath and pressed my hands over my ears, but the screams were so loud you'd have thought the whole world must be able to hear them.

'It's over.' Someone was shaking me. 'It's all right, it's gone quiet. They're all dead now.'

It could not have taken more than ten minutes.

Almost immediately a group of male prisoners approached from the men's camp. These were members of the *Sonderkommando*, who had to shift bodies from the gas chambers into the crematoria and load them into the ovens. Some found themselves burning their own parents or children. The squad numbered two or three hundred, and constantly had to be replaced: most of them committed suicide within a very short time, either by throwing themselves on the electrified fence or by walking into the gas chambers with their friends. Those with stronger stomachs didn't survive much longer, for there were regular routine exterminations to make sure no one remained to tell the tale.

I went on staring at the building. Smoke was beginning to billow out of the tall chimneys. Soon a spurt of flame shot up into the sky. The black smoke became thicker and darker and choking, bringing with it the smell of burning fat and bone and hair. As evening came the whole sky was red. Smoke and flames were pouring out of all the chimneys now.

None of us slept that night.

It was no longer possible to pretend even to yourself that the stories were not really true, could not conceivably be true. All that we had heard and guessed was now here before our eyes. Here were the death factories. In daytime I heard the regular thuds coming from that attractive white house into which people were ushered one at a time with the assurance that they were to be disinfected – thuds which marked successive shots into the head as victims filed through. And day in, day out, we watched the procession towards the gas chambers and heard the screams, and day and night smelt the crematoria as they laboured to keep up with the increasing tempo of incoming transports.

The reason for enlarging the *Kanada Kommando* and our being housed on the site was the stepping-up of the extermination programme. Tens of thousands of Hungarians were due, and Eichmann himself came to study the effectiveness of the 'Special Treatment' devised for them. We all knew something important was happening long before he entered the camp. There was a complete *Lagersperre* whenever any high-ranking official visited, and this day we were shut inside the moment the night shift ended. In the middle of the day I was looking out of the window when a limousine rolled up outside the nearest crematorium. Out stepped a man in civilian clothes whom I had glimpsed once before in S.S. uniform. '*Obersturmbannführer* Eichmann,' whispered one of the girls beside me. He spent some hours in the camp, pacing from one building to another, and inspecting the gas chambers and ovens. Eichmann was not one of those who wanted prisoners kept alive to work in the factories: his one passion was to exterminate as many as possible, as quickly as possible. When he left the camp, the feeling of evil he left behind him was almost as real as the smoke and the stench of burning flesh.

I was on the night shift, so slept and had time off during the day. Day or night there was little rest from the blare of loudspeakers on the station ramp, issuing instructions in one European language after another to new arrivals. 'Leave your belongings where they are. They'll be taken good care of. You will now proceed to showers and disinfection.'

The men unloading baggage or stacking it up on the platform were forbidden under penalty of death to attempt the slightest warning to newcomers. Some nevertheless took great risks, especially when an agitated young mother was separated from her child and tried to rejoin it. By urgent signs or a quickly muttered word or two the men would try to stop her arguing. She must not go with the child, who was doomed to die anyway. She must stay with the living as long as she could. Few understood, and many a mother insisted on staying with her child. The S.S. raised no objections and would allow both to go into the gas chamber. As for the children themselves, those of twelve or thirteen who could pass for being older were urged: 'Say you're eighteen or nineteen, don't let them send you off with the other kids.' Most were too dazed to obey.

When the selection had been made on the ramp and the new arrivals had moved off to work or to die, the male *Kanada* really got down to work. Cases and loose items were distributed between the male and female sorting sheds. Men would wheel the carts into our compound and dump the contents on to heaps which grew higher and higher. Everything was jumbled up except for food, which had to be thrown into one special place known as the Gobble Block.

Girls then brought the stuff on wheelbarrows into the building where we had to sort it out. This was a long wooden shed with benches along either side. Clothes were tipped from the barrows at one end. Each of us had to collect batches of what we were supposed to be parcelling up that day and take them to our position on the bench. A daily quota was laid down. Each bundle had to be taken to the supervisor at the end of the shed so that she could tick off your number and the quantities sorted and packed. We were lucky in our *Kapo*, a very reasonable woman. Some of them loved to stride up and down, picking on some wretched girl at intervals and making her untie a package and start all over again, usually beating her as well.

So really I was helping the Germans by sorting through the possessions of my own kind, right alongside the crematoria where they were being disposed of. By helping to separate valuables and pitiful souvenirs and packing up clothing for distribution among the German population, wasn't I playing the enemy's game?

Mother had urged me to join the *Kanada Kommando*, and after the whole nightmare was over she was the first to reassure me that I had done right: if any of us had refused, others would have been pushed into it. And if by some miracle of communal defiance everyone refused, then the Germans would, you may be sure, have brought in some of their own people. True, this might have kept some able-bodied men away from the front, but would have deprived prisoners of the essential barter material which kept so many alive and provided a few last comforts for those who were going to die anyway. Mother and I always felt it our duty to take as much as possible from the dead and contribute as much as possible to the living.

At one stage I was sorting male jackets. All the pockets had to be emptied – it would never do for some innocent German civilian to find uncomfortable reminders of the previous owner – and often there were photographs among the contents. I never dared look at these. How could I, when a few yards away that very person might at this moment be burning? During another spell, sorting through ladies' underwear, I often found jewellery sewn into seams and corsets. Slit them open, and jewels and gold pieces would pour out. By the end of the session I often had a whole bucketful. Determined to hand in as little as possible, I buried some in the ground near the hut. Banknotes we never handed in: we used them as toilet paper.

With no way of washing our clothes properly, we took every opportunity to change our underwear regularly by substituting our own dirty garments for fresher ones which had recently arrived.

The S.S. woman in charge of *Kanada* suddenly took it into her head that we should all be kitted out in navy blue dresses with white polka dots. We had to dig through vast piles of clothing to find enough of them. Then there was the question of our red crosses. Even the most privileged prisoners had to have these painted on their backs. A *Zugang* was provided with a wide one from shoulder to shoulder, neck to bottom. This gave everyone higher up in the scale the right to beat up the miserable newcomer. As you progressed in your camp career, the red crosses became narrower. Those of us who could now choose our own clothing could also wear only a small cross painted on with lipstick or nail varnish.

Our superior was absurdly proud of herself for smartening us up: we made such a pretty picture on the lawn. There really was a lawn between our block and the crematorium fence. It was kept neatly mown and trimmed as a showpiece, and we were part of that showpiece. Seeing us lying there in our off-duty hours, reasonably dressed, on a well-kept stretch of grass, those filing towards the gas chambers felt reassured. We must have looked so normal and relaxed to them. How could anything be amiss if girls like us were sprawling in the sun, or singing and playing games? Because we did sing and play games. Four of us had come together in one of the little 'families' which sprang up in every block, however shortlived. There were Isa, Jola, 'Ruda' (Ginger) and myself. Two of us worked sorting clothes, the others spent most of their time in the food section. This way we could organize most effectively on one another's behalf. And when we had free time to spend on the lawn we devised ridiculous charades, and with the rest of the girls even staged a three-act play. Sometimes the orchestra from the men's camp came over to play for us.

Yet while all this was going on, those long processions trailed from the ramp to the gas chambers, and even our singing and play-acting could not drown the screams. Smoking chimneys made the air black and heavy with soot. And there was the smell. But to preserve your sanity you had to tell yourself that whatever was happening on the other side of the fence was in fact not happening at all. After a while the sheer numbers dulled any sense of reality. We laughed and sang with red, reeking hell all round us; I even had books to read, found while sorting the bundles.

The camp authorities were anxious to keep order and avoid panic. Disposing of Jews was just a job; the less fuss the better. Keep them moving placidly, slaughter them as you would slaughter beasts in an abattoir, carve off the pieces you need, and dispose of what's left. At all costs avoid a stampede.

Ought we to have shouted out and warned those children, and the stumbling sick and older men and women? We would all have been shot out of hand or tacked on to the end of the death column. And we might have caused unnecessary suffering to those who still did not quite appreciate what was in store for them. Better to go to death with all the dignity of ignorance than in screaming terror. The screams and terror came only right at the end, and then not for long.

Occasionally someone would call across to us. 'Do you girls work in these factories?' They would point to the crematoria, and all we could do was wave back. 'What's being *made* in those factories?'

Women passed us, tired from the journey, clutching their babies. Sometimes a small child wheeled a doll in a little pram or jumped over a skipping rope. A mother would change a nappie or put a bonnet over a child's head if the sun was too hot. We lay on the lawn and watched. Or looked away. One of our group might get up to look behind the block to see what was happening at another of the crematoria. No need.

'They're burning now. Can't you smell it?'

The wind would blow the smoke our way, making us cough and choke, darkening the sun. That lovely baby we had seen not so long ago, the little boy playfully running backwards and forwards, were gone now.

One day when we were on the lawn a small transport of men went past. They looked thin and starved and had obviously not come here straight from home or any 'free' place.

'Where from?' one of us called out.

They were from the Lodz ghetto. And all at once Ginger began to run up and down. She had recognized her father. She ran wildly to the *Blockälteste*, who shook her head in fear. Nothing to be done. Ginger ran to our *Kapo*. She took the risk of hurrying off to speak to the S.S. man on duty. But it was a waste of time.

'None of these *Muselmanns* is any use to us. Too weak for work. Waste of time feeding them.' The men were going straight to Crematorium II without selection. 'If she wants her father, she can join him.'

Ginger stood staring at Crematorium II until the red flames began to leap out of the chimneys. She went on standing and staring for hours.

We couldn't get her away. Then suddenly she started laughing and crying, singing and shouting. She had gone mad. The next day she was found on the fence, dead. Part of my mind urged me to do the same. It was much easier to do it here than in the main camp. There were no trenches and no guards to keep you away from the fence. But either I lacked Ginger's courage, or there was still some knot of stubbornness deep inside which refused to let me take that way out.

It was not until May 1944 that I got the chance to visit my mother again and smuggle some things back into Camp BIIb. Our *Kapo* arranged that every other week a party of about a dozen girls should take a cartload of 'third rate' clothing to the main camp sauna, since it was no use to the Germans. We all saw great possibilities in this, and all of us wanted to be on the party. I managed more trips than most, being by now an 'old number', respected because I had survived so long. Also I had a mother to visit, which none of the others could claim; and strangely I developed toothache once more, and had to renew my dental treatment.

Mother was delighted to see me. I was determined never to come here from *Kanada* empty-handed. I usually wore at least three of every-thing except shoes. I pinned towels inside my dress and carried small articles such as soap and tins of food all along the sleeves. On one occasion I got hold of a large tin of meat which I simply had to smuggle through. But wherever I tried to hide it, it bulged. The only way was to place it between my thighs, which made walking pretty unpleasant. All the same, I was set on getting it into the camp. I hobbled as far as the main gate before anyone suspected anything. I was limping through when I had the feeling of being watched. My heart stopped. There was *Lagerführer* Hössler himself, coming towards me and brusquely asking what was the matter with me.

I couldn't speak. But somebody said: 'She slipped on the way here and hurt her leg, *Herr Lagerführer*.'

'*Ja geh schon du alte Kuh!*' he bellowed at me.

How I got as far as my mother's block I just do not know. But I made it, and it felt wonderful to have outdone them once again.

Inevitably there came a day when I was caught. All because of a small tin of sardines which made a suspicious bulge at my waist. It was the venomous S.S. woman Haase who triumphantly pulled the tin out.

'Ah, so you're in business again? I'll give you business. Here – a present for you.' She hammered her fist into my face. I was dazed, and waited for something worse, but she didn't bother to search me further. In her worst moods she was known to strip prisoners naked, and if she found anything, or even if she just felt like it, she took their numbers.

This invariably meant special punishment such as transfer to the S.K. or an outside work party.

Once I was stopped by Dr Rohde. I thought he must have spotted something and was about to consign me to the death chamber. But it was just that he wanted blood. Not for his experiments this time, but for the benefit of soldiers fighting for the Fatherland. They despised our Jewish blood yet found it good enough to mix with theirs in an emergency.

Although life in *Kanada* might have been the envy of other prisoners, we were still subject to the hatred and random punishments of the S.S. Once when someone in the men's camp had been caught writing a letter to a woman, he and his block-mates were made to perform physical jerks to the whip and commands of S.S. man Wagner. We could glimpse this *Sport* through the fence between our two compounds.

'*Los! Auf! Schneller! Laufen! Nieder! Los! Auf!*'

Men were sitting down, getting up, running, lying on their bellies, all at tremendous speed. If anyone faltered for a second, Wagner was upon him, beating and kicking and still yelling his orders. Men panted, sweat ran down their faces, they trod over each other and trod on those who had finally collapsed. This went on for several hours until Wagner himself was worn out.

The long hut in which we worked had an extension which was used by S.S. men and women. I discovered this one night when I had finished my quota and slunk away without being noticed for a quiet nap behind a load of jumble. Even if you had finished the work, and finished it satisfactorily, you were not allowed to go back to the block to sleep; but with more than 100 girls in that one room, you could easily disappear. In our own little 'family' we worked it turn and turn about, with one of us resting while the others looked busy and lulled suspicion. While taking my turn behind the thick screen of dead people's effects, I became aware of S.S. women drinking and smoking on the other side of the wooden wall. I kept quiet, idly watching them through gaps in the planking, but not really paying much attention.

Unfortunately I made the mistake of supposing they never bothered to return this scrutiny. One day I concealed myself in the usual spot and wrote a letter to my mother on stolen, forbidden paper with a stolen, forbidden pencil. It was not my turn to go on the party visiting the main camp, so I wanted to send the letter with one of the other girls. Of course she would have to be bribed. Bribery was the only valid currency in Auschwitz. Even our *Kapo* had to be given regular handouts to keep her sweet. Inducements like this were possible because although the *Kapo* was in charge of a squad of sorters, she herself was officially allowed no access to the material we sorted. So we filched a bit here, a bit there, and bribed her; she in turn bribed the minor S.S., who were also not allowed near all that loot. We had to be wary during such transactions. The S.S. you could bribe were rarely the true Germans. The best targets were those uniformed but non-Reich collaborators who took part in selections, did guard duty, and supervised gas-chamber procedures because this meant extra rations of food and vodka. Even then their rations were small, and they could easily be corrupted by offers of extras from the wealth of that huge black market, perhaps the biggest in occupied Europe. These toadies accepted more and more bribes as they grew less optimistic about the Nazis' chances of winning. There was even an instance, I discovered much later, of some Ukrainians whose disillusion was such that after a fairly short period as Auschwitz guards they ran off with their arms and ammunition. But they didn't get far.

Anyway, emerging from my hiding place with my letter, I was all set to go through the usual procedure when S.S. man Bedarf stormed in and announced that he had seen me through one of the cracks. He took my number and went out. I was sure that number would be called out first thing in the morning; and it was such a short walk from here to the gas chamber.

Our *Kapo* stuck her neck out yet again. 'She was only writing to her mother, *Herr Sturmbannführer.*'

'What difference does it make who she writes to? It's strictly forbidden, isn't it? *Verboten.*'

But there was a slight difference. Writing to a man could have meant immediate death. But to my mother . . . ? 'She's a political prisoner,' the *Kapo* urged. 'So is her mother. And how many people have mothers in here? A very special case, those two.'

Bedarf wavered. In the end he announced that the whole block would do three hours' *Sport* in the morning. I had got away lightly. But the rest of the girls were none too pleased, and although our *Kapo* had pleaded for me she didn't hesitate to give me a hiding.

It was through the same gaps in that wall that we got the sense of something terrifying building up. Instead of the wireless and gramophone records of songs such as *Wie schön ist das Leben* – How lovely is life – we heard a hushed, feverish muttering. And great preparations were being made outside. In addition to the large pits in front of the crematoria, trenches were being dug on the fringes of the area. Logs and brushwood were being carted in and stacked up. Everything pointed to a large-scale burning. Had they run out of gas? Did they now intend to burn their victims alive?

We took it in turns to watch and listen. The reason for Eichmann's visits became clear. The camp administration had a problem on its hands. Berlin had ordered upwards of 400,000 Hungarian Jews to be shipped in and disposed of within six weeks. The Red Army was pushing its way into Hungary, and still the country had not been purged of Jews. They had to be rushed to destruction – and all this on top of the everyday extermination schedule. Experts had been brought in to supervise the relining of ovens and strengthening of chimneys, but still an additional 10,000 bodies a day was a problem.

One morning at ten o'clock the first of the trains was unloaded. We could see masses of people standing and waiting. We saw them being divided into two groups. One lot were led to the white house, past the little wood and the pretty flower beds. The others passed our fence and lawn on the way to Crematorium III. The column stretched as far as the eye could see. Mothers were clutching children, the men looked bewildered and some of them slightly apprehensive. But some were smiling and chatting, shrugging their shoulders as they discussed how to make the best of a baffling situation. The notices did not alarm them: *To disinfection*. Nobody seemed to notice while queueing for this 'disinfection' that the first batch from their convoy was already dead and burning. How could they not hear the screams? *We* heard them. And what did they make of the smoke and stench pouring out of the chimneys? Perhaps it was so far beyond their comprehension that they shut off a part of their mind and senses.

Smoke gushing out of the crematoria mingled with smoke rising from pits and trenches dug in the ground. Inside our block the air became so black and foul that we opened a window, which only made it worse. And the sound was far worse than the screams to which we had hardened ourselves. This time it was the screaming of thousands in agony, quite different from the muffled retching and howling of those hit by gas. There was no respite now. No selections on the ramp. Just a continuous, insane conveyor belt of human beings.

One of our girls was shrieking along with the victims. 'Don't you see? You know why they're making that noise ... it's different ... they're being roasted alive.'

It was true. There was no time even for the mercies of Zyklon B before the burning. Hundreds were being thrown alive into the specially dug, blazing pits. On top of them went corpses with which the crematoria could not cope. Bodies from the gas chambers lay stacked up waiting their turn. All night the arc lamps shone down as the *Sonderkommando* dragged consignments of the dead off tip-up lorries and fed them into the open pyres. Even the S.S. men on the ramp and in charge of the columns within the gates had to be fortified with extra alcohol rations. Days and nights of hell and sweat, of smoke and smouldering human remains. No place to hide from the smell, nowhere to run to. Ginger was lucky. She had gone mad and finished herself off. I felt I was going mad. We were all mad. It was the only sensible thing to be. Someone in the block made up a dance and called it 'Under the Smoking Chimneys'. Each day at least 20,000 people passed us on their way to death. And all the time great loads of clothes and food and diamonds poured into the *Kanada* compound. We were almost smothered. Every day the lorries went off full of loot for the glory of the German Reich.

Men of the *Sonderkommando* were throwing themselves in increasing numbers on to the fence or walking into the gas chambers. Some of our girls who had withstood the horror so far could take it no longer, and joined the men on the fence. They were immediately replaced. More and more workers were assigned to *Kanada*. Like us, they had to learn to be numb, deaf and blind.

On some of our trips back to the main camp our *Kapo* and the S.S. woman in charge took us a longer way round instead of cutting across by the usual route. This was largely for the S.S. woman's own benefit: she fancied a spell away from the fences, and a stroll through more open countryside. We soon learned to dread this. It was no invigorating country walk as far as we were concerned. In order to reach more open ground we had to pass close to the pits where corpses were being thrown into the flames, and often the living as well. We were forbidden to look. Anyone who turned her head was liable to be pulled out of line and consigned to those pits herself. But still we couldn't help risking quick glances, and from the corners of our eyes were always aware of the smoke and glare and blazing bodies, raked over from time to time by men of the *Sonderkommando* so that a steady draught could fan the flames.

Nevertheless, I wanted to be on the party as often as possible in order to see my mother. Because of this I lost my back teeth at an early age. I managed several visits on the old excuse of my toothache, and also got the dentist to extract those teeth in which my father had arranged to insert diamonds while we were in Lublin. It was a painful business, as there was no anaesthetic. When I left I took the diamonds away in the seam of my sleeve. Even if I had been searched there was little chance of the well-covered diamonds being detected; the searcher would simply have thought I was a bit mad to want to hoard old teeth. So many people in that place were mad, one way and another, that it would have aroused no comment.

In the middle of all this there developed the only relationship I ever knew of between an S.S. man and a Jewish girl. Some ridiculous misconceptions have been passed around by folk with prurient imaginations. One popular myth is that numbers of Jewish women prisoners were employed in S.S. brothels. I never once heard of any such thing, then or later. At all times it was punishable by death for a Reich German to associate with a Jewess. Such women were fit only to be enslaved, beaten up and massacred, certainly not to have intimate physical contact with the master race. The S.S. brothel was supplied from other sources, including German political prisoners and civil criminals. As for the hurried sex between male and female prisoners, there was no chance, ever, of any lasting relationship. I believe that in the male compounds some younger boys stood a better chance of survival if they became the pets of privileged male prisoners. They were protected and received food in return for their favours. In our *Kanada* group we were indirectly granted some concessions by the S.S. officer in charge of stores, an Austrian named Wünsch who fell genuinely in love with a Hungarian girl. She had managed in spite of everything to stay attractive. Several of us stood guard while the two of them made love behind heaps of goods waiting to be sorted; and in return '*Wiener Schnitzel*', as we nicknamed him, treated us fairly well.

But such concessions bought from one man did not make up for what his fellows were doing. Somehow we had to revenge those who had died, and the 20,000 who were dying every day. Someone, sometime, had to strike back. Beneath our numbness there was a bottled-up hatred; but there was nothing we could do about it. There was less and less talk nowadays of 'when we get out, what shall we do with *them* . . . and ourselves?' Even rumours about the tide of war turning against the Nazis aroused little optimism. We feared the world outside would never know the truth, for when we were no further use to the Germans our turn would come, and then all traces of what went on here would be wiped away.

One afternoon while we were inside the sauna taking showers (another of the luxuries of *Kanada*) there was a strong smell of gas. Was it perhaps our imagination? Or was it the end, just as we had half expected all along? Everyone ran for the door, terrified in case it was bolted. I got out naked. Outside the smell was even stronger. Choking and coughing, we ran back in. Some fainted from shock. It would have been quite like them to have taken us by surprise. In fact it turned out that the doors of one of the gas chambers had been opened too soon and gas had escaped into the camp.

It often happened that when the doors were opened too early some

A selection taking place: those capable of work being led off; older ones facing immediate death (an S.S. photograph)

Sleeping quarters in Block 20, a stone hut with a mud floor

Interior of a lavatory hut in the women's camp, specially photographed for me by the Auschwitz Museum

The interior of a hospital block, one of the wooden huts

A visit by Heinrich Himmler (left) to Auschwitz's first commandant, Rudolf Höss

A canister of Zyklon B poison gas crystals

Kanada I at work sorting gas victims' jumbled possessions to be taken into various huts for packing and despatch (an S.S. photograph)

Return to Auschwitz: crying on the ramp by the railway lines inside the camp. This is where transports of new arrivals were off-loaded

Above: Saying goodbye before leaving for England: myself and my mother with two uniformed Quaker relief workers on either side and my friend Henia between us

people were still alive. Once, to the horror of the men in the *Sonder-kommando*, a tiny baby was found still sucking at its mother's breast. It had probably been sucking all the time and so had not inhaled the deadly fumes. S.S. man Wagner was furious. He snatched the baby away and threw it into a blazing oven.

Once I had been able to get a considerable number of valuables back to the main camp. A party of men had come to do some work on drums in the basement of the sauna, only a few hours after I had found a large quantity of watches, diamonds and other jewellery which I was anxious to get rid of before a search. I went into the sauna and approached the S.S. man who guarded the men to prevent them from speaking to the girls.

'*Herr Sturmbannführer*,' I said, 'please may I bring the men some of our *Lagersuppe*?'

He hesitated, eyeing me suspiciously, but then said: 'Go on, but hurry up about it.'

I ran back to our party and we quickly poured some soup into a bucket, then dropped the jewellery in. The problem was to let the men know so that they wouldn't choke on the contents. I hung around until the S.S. man turned his head for a second, then made frantic signs. They understood, and I was delighted to think of those riches going into the camp. The greater the influx of loot, the more we tried to steal and pass along.

We didn't really believe mutterings about a Resistance movement within the camp; yet we had to believe *something*. If only word could be got out to the world . . . and sabotage material brought in.

One day there was great excitement. Someone burst into our hut while we were fast asleep. 'Girls, something terrific has happened. Mala, the messenger, has run away. She's actually got out.'

Mala Zimmelbaum was a nineteen-year-old Belgian who was rumoured to have been with the Belgian Resistance. She spoke several languages, and was spared immediate gassing in order to act as inter-preter. As *Läuferin*, or messenger, she worked hard in the interests of her fellow prisoners. She also managed the perilous business of carrying on an affair with a Pole whose administrative job allowed him some freedom to move about. Together they decided to escape and spread the news of what was going on inside the extermination camps.

There were immediate searches through the camp, savage beatings, wild attempts to pin the blame on scores of innocent inmates. The entire camp was made to pay. But it was worth it. If the two of them could tell the world outside, could somehow get through to the Allies, then surely action would be taken.

Some weeks later all prisoners were driven out of their blocks, and we in *Kanada* were recalled to the main camp. They wanted us all to see Mala, beaten and bloody. And they wanted to hang her in front of us, as a lesson. The S.S. leaders, several of whom had liked her and admired her efficiency, were there to watch the ceremony.

At the very moment she was to be hanged, Mala suddenly pulled out a razor blade and cut her wrists. An S.S. man made a grab at her. '*Was machst du*, Mala?'

'Don't touch me,' she shouted back. 'Filthy dog. Murderer! Murderers!'

She collapsed in a pool of blood. *Oberführerin* Drechsler began to shriek at her. 'You thought you'd get away? Cheat the German Reich? We get everyone in the end – *everyone*, you see?'

They loaded her on to a hand-cart and ordered some of her friends to push it along the *Lagerstrasse* so that everyone could see. And then she was to go straight to the crematorium. We hoped and prayed she would be dead before she got there: they obviously had every intention of burning her alive. As she went, she managed one last cry. 'It doesn't matter, your days are numbered. You're going to die, you swine, all of you.'

Back among the smoking chimneys, a small transport of about 300 girls had arrived from Majdanek, a concentration camp far inside Poland. They looked unusually well and healthy as they were led to the sauna, perhaps to be attached immediately to the *Kanada Kommando*. Our own girls working in there were able to have a few words with them. 'So you'll register us and number us, if we're to go into the camp,' said one of the newcomers. 'Unless they decide to take us there.' She pointed to the crematoria.

'What on earth are you talking about?'

'Oh, you needn't try to deceive us, we know it all. We worked in the *Kanada Kommando* in Majdanek sorting belongings of the dead, just as you're doing here. We're not afraid of the truth.'

Apparently when the Red Army was approaching Majdanek there was a general roll-call within the camp. All 15,000 inmates had then been machine-gunned with the exception of these 300, who had been left alive to strip the corpses and sort their belongings for despatch to the Third Reich. They could not believe they would survive very long for they, like us, were witnesses of so much slaughter. We all breathed again when they had been shaved and numbered in the usual way, and so made ready for the camp.

Next morning news reached us from the *Sonderkommando*. During the night two lorries had been brought to the new girls' block. All 300 of them had been loaded and taken to the gas chambers. So even the most experienced had been taken by surprise.

Very shortly afterwards the men of the *Sonderkommando* were informed that they were to go 'on transport' and be sent to another camp. They were doubtful. Was it just another trap set up by those cowards, who wanted at all costs to avoid panic and trouble? And what awaited them even if they did move away? They were apprehensive and hopeful at the same time; everyone so much liked to cling to every scrap of hope. The men vowed they would not let themselves be taken alive if there was any hint of trickery. Secret messages were smuggled into other camps. Everyone waited for something to happen. It was thought that the men would attack the S.S. as soon as they were well on their way, or at the first sign of anything going wrong. They were smiling as they marched past our block, determined to fight. On they marched towards the headquarters camp of Auschwitz I to be deloused and reclothed before setting off for another camp. You could almost sense the joy they felt as they put greater and greater distance between themselves and the hell of smoking chimneys.

The *Bekleidungskammer*, or clothing stores, in Auschwitz was in an ordinary block just like all the others. The men of the *Sonderkommando* were in the middle of changing into fresh clothes when suddenly the doors were bolted and gas was let in. They died within a few minutes, just as thousands of others had done before them in the gas chambers. They had been convinced that this time they would detect any underhand methods; they knew them all. But they, too, had been fooled. It was obvious the S.S. were afraid of a revolt and had tricked them before it could break out. Was this the way all resistance or promised resistance would end?

We kept hiding away valuables and passing them to men on work parties whenever the chance arose. They spoke of an underground movement, but it was risky to trust them. Risky to trust anyone. But we did decide that we had to take the chance of smuggling things out in the hope that they would fall into the right hands. If any items reached the S.S., that would only be as bribery.

We didn't know how long we had. Maybe all our pitiful little contributions were too late, anyway. The Russian advance on Majdanek had led to the swift extermination of all its occupants. We could not tell how long the Russians would take to get to Auschwitz, or how long it would take the S.S. to decide what to do.

9

The Death March

EARLY IN August 1944 there were rumours that the whole Auschwitz complex was to be evacuated. The Red Army must be drawing near, and the Germans had no intention of leaving anyone behind to be liberated.

No fresh transports were arriving. Tension mounted in our section. Soon the S.S. would have no further use for us. More whispers from 'reliable sources' reported that orders had come through from Berlin for gassing to cease. We would have loved to believe that, but we didn't, and when lorries began to arrive suddenly at the crematoria one night we found out how right we were. At first we thought it was a *Transport S.B.* (*Sonder Behandlung* or 'Special Treatment', since it was not polite to use the word 'extermination') bringing patients from the hospital for liquidation. But there were so many of them that you soon got the impression that a full-size camp was being emptied. The truth emerged a couple of days later. The Germans had exterminated the entire gipsy camp, *Lager BIIe*.

We were staggered. That *Familienlager* or Family Camp had been a sort of showcase, photographs of which were released to the international press showing the Children's School and other apparently happy scenes. Unlike most other prisoners the gipsies had been allowed to live with their own families. There had been one other such family grouping: a Czech camp, which had survived with a self-government less vicious than others, apparently tolerated by the S.S. until in June and July 1944 they had liquidated the lot. Now it was the turn of the gipsies.

As non-Jews, they had escaped tattooing and, like political and criminal prisoners, were methodically listed in the camp records. When all 5,000 were gassed during the night of 6 August 1944, some explanation had to be added to those records: after all, how could anyone believe that 5,000 people had died of natural causes in one night? With typical thoroughness the S.S. devised and registered their excuse. About a score of Polish and Jewish prisoner doctors working in the camp were declared responsible for the outbreak of a typhus epidemic which had brought about the death of the gipsies. As a punishment they were transferred to the S.K., the hard labour *Kommando*, and then sent away 'on transport'.

So we were not going to believe tales about an end to gassing. Nor did we believe that the transports beginning to roll away from the camp in increasing numbers were taking people off to work in factories. And as for excited hints about a rebellion, a break-out at last . . . well, that was fantasy of a different kind, but still fantasy.

Although no further trainloads were entering the camp there was still a terrific backlog of stuff to be sorted. We stood a better chance of staying alive as long as the work was incomplete, so we didn't hurry through the piles. Then, late in the afternoon of 7 October, as we were getting ready for our usual shift, there was a change in the atmosphere. Shots began to rattle out from the men's side of the fence. Some of us ran to the windows, some right out of the hut. What a sight! Flames were belching out of Crematorium IV. Within minutes the whole building was on fire. First the roof caved in, then flames began to lick up from the gas chambers. There was an explosion, and a kind of thunder as one huge chimney toppled to the ground. Everywhere there was wild commotion. Was the camp being bombed?

Screams and shouts mingled with the wail of sirens. We couldn't move, not knowing if this was the uprising we'd hardly dared to expect or if we would have to fight with our bare hands or somehow be provided with arms and ammunition. Somebody somewhere had arms – the exchange of fire continued – and from the sound of it there were some grenades going off. Then came another mighty explosion. This one was from Crematorium II. Within minutes the chimneys collapsed. Gas chambers and ovens went up in flame and smoke.

Fire engines were racing into the camp. S.S. motorcycles dashed madly all over the place. The cowards looked really frightened, riding or running up and down and shooting at random. Immediate curfew was ordered, and those of us not already safely inside were soon scuttling for cover in our blocks.

As the flames died down, shooting could be heard from within the shattered crematoria. Machine-gun fire echoed across the lawn. And from the direction of the woods came more firing, where another battle seemed to have flared up near the pits. At last the uproar died down. The victorious S.S. could be seen marching back from their battlefield. There would be no break-out.

In fact this was not what the demonstration had been aimed at. Our stolen valuables had reached Resistance men all right and had been passed on to where they would be of most use. Four girls working in the Krupp *Union Werke* ammunition factory had bribed other workers and minor S.S. so that they could smuggle out explosives. All those slow, spasmodic efforts which I had often thought might be in vain were coming to fulfilment. The Polish Resistance outside had learned through their contacts of the imminent abandonment of Auschwitz by the Germans and the final massacre of the Jews. Men of the *Sonderkommando*, remembering the fate of their immediate predecessors, decided not to wait for their own liquidation but to strike one mighty blow now. It had to be rushed through because their plans were overheard by a 'green' *Kapo*, who they dealt with by throwing him alive into a blazing oven. If that seems hideous, one has only to remember what the usual daily routine of those ovens was.

The destruction of the two crematoria was a wonderful gesture, whatever its other consequences. Bit by bit the details filtered through to us in *Kanada*. In the skirmishes the saboteurs had managed to kill a number of S.S. men and had thrown another of them into the flames alive. Hidden weapons were dug out of their hiding places and turned against the guards. A handful of men were said to have broken out and escaped from the camp, but we had no idea how far they had got.

Now came an enormous inquiry by the camp police. Women from the ammunition factory squads were tortured, and the four girls who had supplied the explosives were soon identified. In spite of even more hideous torture, they refused to give away their contacts, and finally were hanged in full view of the entire camp. After one interminable *Zählappell* we were put on *Sport*, fully expecting it to be followed by a selection for the remaining gas chambers. But apparently we were still of use and had to be kept alive a little longer.

There was mounting talk of complete evacuation. Someone had heard that transports were leaving for Gross-Rosen, Ravensbrück and other concentration camps. And there was a story that factory chiefs had been seen selecting girls for work. Then one morning there were more explosions. It was hard to credit that there still could be caches of explosives which the S.S. had failed to find, or enough determined survivors of the *Sonderkommando* to renew the campaign. Maybe the Russians were here at last. We looked around, saw billowing smoke, and there, not far from us, another crematorium was being destroyed.

It was followed by the fourth, and work parties set about digging up the foundations. This time it was the Germans themselves who were responsible for the demolition. Clearly all traces of the machinery of massacre were to be obliterated.

And after all the buildings were gone, what would happen to us? We were the only witnesses left. If all traces were to be wiped away then it only remained to get rid of us few.

There were new rumours. The S.S. were waiting only for the order from the *Reichssicherheitsamt* in Berlin to dispose of us. There was talk that a bomb would be dropped and explained away as an Allied bomb. We waited. Trainloads continued to leave Auschwitz. But not with any members of the *Kanada Kommando* aboard.

One morning after the usual *Zählappell* there was a call: '*Häftling* 39934, report to the *Kapo* at once.'

My first thought was that something had been found in my bunk and I was due for a whipping. But then came a worse idea: they had found some connection between me and the material used for bribes by the dead *Union Werke* girls. I went to the *Kapo* to learn my fate.

She said: '39934, *Lagerführer* Hössler has ordered your transfer to *Lager BIIb*. You'll be going on transport with your mother.'

It was too good to be true. I couldn't believe my ears. After eight months of nightmare on the edge of the inferno, during which I had seen something like two million people going to their death, I felt I was being sent back from the grave. Still I wondered what gruesome catch there might be in it.

The reason for the decision was as incredible as everything else. Mother had done something which no one else would have dared attempt. She herself would not have risked it during our early days in Auschwitz, but after more than a year and a half she had become a distinguished elderly citizen of the place and could brace herself to speak directly to the commandant. This was of course strictly forbidden. He and his subordinates were taken completely by surprise. Mother simply went up to him on the *Lagerstrasse* and politely said in her best German:

'*Herr Lagerführer*, I would be most grateful if you could get my daughter out of *Kanada*. She has worked there for eight months. I am due to go on transport, and would like her to join me.'

Hössler looked her up and down, then asked for my number. He must have been impressed by her courage and her perfect German; and also by her camp number and mine. They were so old by Auschwitz standards that anyone might marvel at our aptitude for survival.

'We shall see,' he replied at last.

So I was called to rejoin my mother. It was yet another of those crazy incongruities. In one moment of compassion or grudging respect the camp commandant had freed just one person from that doomed *Kommando*. My friends in it must all have been wiped out soon after, for in spite of exhaustive inquiries after the war I have been unable ever to trace one of them still living.

On 11 November 1944 my mother and I were among a special selection of 100, most of them privileged prisoners, to be removed at last from Auschwitz. Mist from the surrounding swamps hung over the whole compound, as usual. But now it was not suffused with smoke from the crematoria. All the millions who had died in here – and I was to leave it alive! Joy was tinged with doubt. The S.S. had deceived us so many times and then gleefully renewed the tortures and humiliations. Could they really be evacuating us? Mother and I were alert for any sign of trickery. At the sauna, for example, where outgoing as well as incoming transports were disinfected as a matter of course. But we did not even go into the sauna. Ours was a transport of 'personalities', excused the shaving and cleansing and even excused a search at the main gate. If only I had known, I could have smuggled so many small valuables out from *Kanada* to help on whatever trip we might be taking, to whatever destination.

At least we were wearing warm clothing, which I had appropriated before leaving. Bread rations were issued outside the gate; a train waited at the siding. My uneasiness returned. I had seen so many trains in that siding. Would they deceive us as they had deceived the gipsies, the girls from Majdanek, the men of the *Sonderkommando*? Everything looked straightforward enough. The engine on the train was headed away from the camp, not towards the crematorium. It was a good sign.

Darkness had fallen by the time we boarded. I turned round for one last look at the place. We had arrived at Auschwitz by night and now we were leaving it by night.

Our train consisted of cattle trucks. Almost as soon as the doors were bolted it became stuffy inside. The only ventilation was through gaps in the floor. It was so crowded that in the pitch blackness we had to grope our way about and sit down in turn, or else sit on top of one another. Hours passed and still we had not moved. Then there was a clank and a jolt. We were moving ... backwards. So they hadn't finished with us, they were just playing with us? In fact the train was merely being shunted to the points. Within a few minutes it was moving forward, gathering speed. We were on our way. As the wheels clattered into a steady rhythm we knew that we must by now be out of the camp area. Some began to cry. I could only laugh; no tears, for my emotions had died long ago. Nothing mattered except that we were going further and further from Auschwitz.

I realized how different things might be at our new destination. We had no idea what we would have to face, but it would surely be better if we could face them together. Into the darkness I said:

'Look, from now on we're all equal. *Kapos*, block leaders, everyone – we all start from scratch. We may not be safe for a long time yet, but remember we're all equal.'

I wondered if I'd gone too far too soon. One of those who had held authority might still automatically make a move to beat me up. But from the middle of the truck the voice of one of them said yes, I was right, we had to work together and try to stay together.

'Friends. Let's all be friends.' We joined hands. Friends . . . after all that time when the mere word had been a mockery!

Time dragged on. I dozed and woke up again, jarred by continual kicks. Legs could not be stretched without poking into someone else. But somehow we had to snatch some sleep.

All at once the train stopped and the doors opened. It was broad daylight. We were almost blinded. It was difficult to tell in which direction we had travelled; for all we knew we might have been going round in circles, and for an instant that was what we thought when we saw fences, still lit up although it was daytime, and watch-towers just like those at Auschwitz. It turned out that there were indeed many people from Auschwitz here. This was Gross-Rosen camp, which had become a transit centre from which transports were leaving daily for unknown destinations. After a night's stay we were joined by another 100 girls and led back into the cattle trucks. The train travelled further west. Once again it was only a short journey and then we came to a sudden halt. The doors opened and we found ourselves in the middle of a field.

'*Alles raus! Alles raus! Anstellen, schneller verfluchte Bande*' – the familiar shouts and language of the S.S. and their minions greeted us.

We were marched off in the usual fives. After about an hour the familiar outlines of fences, sentry boxes and a main gate appeared on the horizon. Yet another camp. And would there be chimneys, too?

A *Lagerälteste* awaited us. And a *Blockälteste*, to take us into a hut. It was hard to believe the tales we had heard of the German army falling back everywhere. Here the pattern was much as it had always been: the same hierarchy, the same rules and regulations and threats of dire punishment. And there were the same bunk beds, but here at least we found an improvement: only two to a bed! Also, there were only 100 to the hut, and all of us from Auschwitz had been lodged together.

There were real toilets and we were even allowed to use cold water taps in the washroom. Still there was one thing we wanted to know. Any gas chambers? Girls who had been there some time had never heard of them.

The camp was a small one, some two hours' walk from the town of Reichenbach in south-east Germany. We did that walk every morning and evening, allocated to work in a Telefunken factory which had manufactured radio sets before the war but now produced war materials. As everything was top secret it was hard to guess just what the place was producing.

Reveille was still at four o'clock in the morning; the sacred roll-call was still the same; our bread ration was just as it had been in Auschwitz. But the walk, though long, took us not through mud and desolation but in part through the centre of the town. It did us good to see real houses and real streets with proper pavements, even though we were not allowed to walk on these. We looked forward especially to passing a bakery from which came wonderful smells of freshly baked loaves. Our hunger was acute, for apart from soup and our bread ration we got nothing: there was no way of 'organizing' things, the way we had learned to do in Auschwitz. All the same it was marvellous to smell those beautiful loaves and go on seeing them in our dreams.

Trudging through the snow was no fun, and we had to hunt around for any scraps of paper we could find to wrap our legs against frostbite. But once in the factory, we were warm. Such comfort was not specifically for our benefit; it was for the German civilians beside whom we had to work. We were not permitted to talk to these civilians, and after what we had been through we were not particularly anxious to do so anyway. It was obvious that they, too, were afraid to speak or even to look at us. We all went on with our jobs while S.S. women patrolled the factory floor to make sure there was no contact.

I was placed next to a German girl at a control panel with numerous dials and meters. At the back of the panel was a kind of gas stove into which glass was blown in the shape of a bulb, and underneath it a cylinder of what I imagined must be carbon dioxide. Part of my job was to replace these cylinders when necessary, and no one told me this could be a dangerous procedure. Like ice to the touch, the stuff in fact burned when brought into contact with the skin. One day a cylinder overflowed and burned my arm right through my clothes. The girl next to me saw what had happened and called the foreman over. He ran to the S.S. woman on duty, but she told both of them to mind their own business.

My arm turned septic, and was in an awful state for some weeks before healing up. The incident shook my German neighbour, who began to risk glancing at me from time to time and whispering sympathetic questions about my burn. Maybe until then she had not realized how cruel her own people could be. One day she put one of her lunch sandwiches to one side when nobody was looking, and nodded at me to hide it. After that she left a daily sandwich for me in a special spot, and any time the S.S. woman went off for a few minutes, perhaps to the lavatory, I'd get a quick smile and some friendly remarks.

When the civilians wanted to go to the lavatory, they went. For us there were set times during which whole squads were marched off and the guards kept watch outside. In spite of that, it is amazing what we managed to achieve in such short respites. There was warm water in the lavatories, and we used it for hurried baths – or the nearest thing we could manage. In the factory there were any number of shallow trays used for carrying screws and small parts. Between us we could smuggle these into the lavatory one at a time, and then three or four of us would splash ourselves frenziedly from head to foot with the water.

Back in the camp there was no warmth. Many of us had left Auschwitz in reasonable shape – Mother from the hospital compound, me from *Kanada*, and the others after reasonable pickings as privileged prisoners – but now we had dismal rations and freezing cold living conditions. Among our consolations, however, was the fact that we were usually left in peace after evening *Zählappell*. This meant we could talk and share out whatever meagre extras any of us had been able to organize. I would bring back my daily sandwich and divide it between my mother and myself. Some of the girls picked up a few scraps from other sympathetic civilians; and one very daring Auschwitz survivor, Marta, found a remarkable source of supply. An expert thief, she always insisted on walking on the outside of the row of fives during the journey to work, and could lift the lunches out of S.S. women's pockets without their feeling the slightest thing. They must have been bewildered and suspicious at the regularity of this, but not once was she caught. The trouble was, she was such an instinctive thief that during the night she stole from her hut mates, too. Bread rations vanished from under our mattresses, though we never actually found her eating it. And although I prided myself on my alertness, one night my only jumper disappeared. Later I saw her wearing it but never managed to get it back, so had to go on freezing.

It was a bitterly cold winter, with huge drifts of snow. There was nobody on duty to forbid us having a fire in the stove, so we managed to warm the heating channel by removing a slat of wood a time from each of our bunks in turn, smashing it up and feeding it into the flames. A few 'organized' potatoes were heated and for a while the hut was warm. Gradually it grew more and more uncomfortable to sleep on what remained of the slats.

One night, just as we had got the fire lit, an S.S. woman came in and demanded to know where the wood had come from. An immediate inspection showed the gaps in the bunks, and the whole block was punished: no food for the next twenty-four hours. In addition the woman picked out one girl and ordered her hair to be completely shaved off. This was Henia, a girl who had held quite a responsible post in Auschwitz but since our departure had been one of the happiest to accept the new idea of equality. The strain on her in the camp must have been enormous, and to be able to relax among friends had made a world of difference to her outlook. Already she was one of my closest and staunchest friends. She had the most beautiful hair, which was probably why she had been singled out. We were all miserable and angry on her behalf.

Work in the Telefunken factory went on for nearly four months until, early in February 1945, we began to hear distant gunfire. Nobody was supposed to pay any attention, but we listened and waited for it to come nearer. Every day it grew louder, until it was plain that this was not just a series of bombing raids on various targets but the steady advance of ground armies. The Soviet troops were closing in from the east. When the gunfire grew so loud that it was obvious Reichenbach had been occupied, we did not set out for our usual daily walk to work. That night we joked and sang. This time we must surely be liberated.

Without warning the S.S. burst into our hut.

'*Zählappell. Alles raus, sofort anstellen. Marschbefehl.*'

How stupid to suppose the Germans would leave us behind to regain our freedom. The entire camp population assembled outside, several thousand of us altogether, and the *Lagerälteste* told us we were to be evacuated at once. All the main roads were either in Allied hands or choked by German military convoys. There was only one road left towards the west, and this went over a mountain pass. We were to be taken away at all costs.

By now my priorities were established: I made sure my tin mug was securely fastened to a string round my waist and kept close to my mother. Our own special group formed up around us. The date sticks in my mind. We had caught up with the calendar again in recent months, and this was 18 February, my mother's birthday. It was still pitch dark as we faced the Eulengebirge mountain range, but with a pale smudge of dawn in the eastern sky. 'So as a birthday present,'

Mother commented wryly, 'I'm to be treated to a walk up in the hills!'

We set off in a long, straggling column with no idea where we were going. The guards did not seem much wiser. Many of them were ex-soldiers of the *Wehrmacht* rather than trained S.S., and looked past retiring age. But their orders were clear enough. Anyone who fell by the wayside was not to be left behind alive: they would be clubbed to death or shot.

Our progress was so slow that we hoped the Russians might over-take us, but either they had other things to do or we were going in a different direction. We seemed to be heading south for a while. As we went, our column was increased by prisoners collected from every side until there must have been well over 10,000. When we began to climb uphill we walked into steady snow, making the ground wet and slippery. Most of us were tired after only a few hours and even the guards looked exhausted; but that served them right. My feet ached, and in spite of the cold I was hot and sweaty. Soon I threw away my coat, and then the blanket from my bunk which I had thought would come in handy. It was impossible to carry anything of any weight.

Some of the Auschwitz girls began to lag behind. Mother was among them. I fell back, and with Henia and several of the others urged them to stay with us and keep going. Once we were scattered it would be difficult to find one another again. Anyone in our group who lagged had to be coaxed and bullied into keeping up. We lent an arm to those who wanted to abandon the struggle, and even took turns to carry some of them short distances. We couldn't give up after persevering for so long. When the snow thinned there was brilliant sunshine. The mountain range was dazzling. We tried to admire it, tried to talk and sing; anything to distract us from the misery of aching bones and empty stomachs.

Another burden with which we were saddled was the guards' belongings. We had to share out their boxes and provisions among us. On the way a few morsels of food were organized from these loads, and some items were surreptitiously ditched in the snow. Already some of the girls were falling by the wayside. Our singing faltered and stopped as we saw half a dozen being clubbed to death with rifle butts, or heard the occasional shot from further back down the line.

Snow clouds were thickening more ominously on the summit of the Grosse Eule (the Great Owl), the highest peak in these parts. We were supposed to get right up there by nightfall, but this was im-possible; nor could we see why it should be so important to reach the top.

At intervals the guards called a halt for collective manuring of the landscape. You were not allowed to stop on your own and then catch up when you had finished.

'Halt!' would come the shout, echoing away down the column. 'You can perform.'

The guards had to watch us at it unless they chose to turn away. It couldn't have been a particularly enticing sight for them. When they performed, they took it in turns to go behind trees or into the occasional hut or cottage by the side of the track, but we had no such privacy. It didn't matter. By then we had lost all shyness, and in fact flaunted our bottoms at them as a punishment. These stops provided a useful opportunity for the Auschwitz girls to reassemble and round up the stragglers.

We spent the night some way below the summit. The ground was frozen hard and there was no shelter. We had suffered from snow and cold often enough in Auschwitz, but there at least we had been under cover at night. Many girls had died by morning.

What was the use of plodding on towards a destination which might not even exist? The guards had no idea how far we had to go or what the future was for any of us. No food, no shelter. Would it be worth while trying to run away? But how far could you get with a number on your arm, shaven hair, prison dress with a red cross on the back, and no identity papers? And no shoes, for already our shoes had been worn through, and most of us had wrapped rags round our blistered, tattered feet.

As the sun rose we continued to climb. All at once we reached the summit – and what a sight greeted us there on top! I don't know whether we'd expected to find a steep slope down the other side of the range, or even a precipice. What we had certainly not been ready for was this wide plateau, bathed in morning sunshine, with hundreds of people placidly eating breakfast, some on the ground and others under the hoods of horse-drawn carts. In some of the carts, whole families were still half asleep. All around were groups of cows.

Our Auschwitz group was in the vanguard. It took us only a few seconds to sum up the situation. Food! We threw ourselves at the terrified animals, who bolted in all directions. I made a desperate grab at the biggest of them all, and got such a kick in the stomach that I was thrown several yards.

Mother came rushing up. 'What possessed you, trying to milk that one?'

'It looked the biggest,' I whimpered.

'You can't milk a bull!'

Together we lunged at the next cow, a real one this time. Furiously and inexpertly I managed to get some drops of warm milk into my mug. Mother and I shared it, gulping it down. It was a blissful feeling.

People were scrambling up from the ground. Those in the carts woke up and stared. One of us noticed a string of sausages dangling from the side of one cart, and ten of us rushed for them and began pulling them apart. By this time guards were running across the meadow and yelling, but there were so many goggle-eyed civilians everywhere that they hesitated to shoot us. The families began to run away. The drivers of the carts lashed their horses in a panic. It did us good to see these fleeing Germans. For a change they were the refugees, running away from the fast approaching Russians – farmers escaping with their livestock and such food as they could load on to their carts. It was their turn now.

The guards were trying to hustle us away towards a wide track descending the other side of the range, but the column had not finished coming up to the edge of the plateau, so in the confusion we grabbed what we could from the slow-moving carts before they got away. I loosened a bucket from one of them and it turned out to be a bucket of lard. We ate some of it, and smeared our bodies with the rest.

'Here – try this on your feet.'

'Beauty treatment, Henia . . .'

From the summit of the Grosse Eule we began a descent which took us for a while through the border country of the Czech Sudetenland. At last we were on the flat again, trudging along a country road past farms and through small villages. A few girls deserted and hid in the farms in the hope of escape, but most of us didn't fancy risking ourselves on territory still under German control, with no way of telling what the local situation was.

We did go into farms from time to time, however. No food had been issued, and we were desperate. Under cover of darkness little groups of us raided the farms and took whatever could be snatched up. It was even possible to manage these brief expeditions in daylight, if you were sharp about it. Those of us walking at the front could raid a farm and rejoin the column without too much trouble, and then at the first stop we would rejoin our own group and share out the spoils. Any cow we came across in a meadow was liable to find herself milked, whether it was her usual time or not. We found eggs in chicken houses, and fair quantities of raw potatoes, beets and cabbages.

On the third day of the pilgrimage we were passing through villages where Germans were getting ready to leave for the west. Some local farmers were still driving cartloads of produce along the road, and as soon as one came in sight we in the Auschwitz group got ready and, when we were almost level, threw ourselves on the cart and grabbed whatever came to hand. The guards lashed out with their rifle butts, but there were too few of them to stop us.

The weather stayed bright and dry for several days, with only the occasional snowstorm. We passed through the most beautiful country, and in spite of our aches and weariness we could not help enjoying the woods and lakes basking in the cold sunlight. Those who foraged for food were better able to enjoy the landscape: it was a case of grab or starve, and those who lacked the will to raid farms and carts also lacked the will to appreciate their surroundings, and in the end lacked strength to go on at all.

Our column became shorter and shorter. At the same time it was becoming more disorganized. When one of the guards handed me a case of his belongings to carry, I fell back so that I could walk behind him, emptied the case into a ditch as we staggered along, and then passed it down the column. It was now empty – and light. We played a sort of grotesque game of 'pass the parcel', nobody wanting to be the one left with the empty case when the guard wished to reclaim it. It was a sign of their own growing exhaustion that the guards themselves were too dazed to make an issue of such things and seemed almost at the end of their tether.

'Got any spare lard for the poor old guard's feet?'

'Come on, help the poor old chap along.'

We could dare to joke without much fear of reprisals. The guards themselves were mumbling and complaining, cursing 'this damned trudge', and still appeared to have no idea where we would end up. But every now and then one would lose his temper and take out his frustrations on one of us. One afternoon I made a dash at a cart laden with potatoes. I was expert by now in these raiding tactics, but this time a guard really went for me with his rifle. Other girls swarmed over the cart and got away. I was the one to get the butt of the weapon right across my head, knocking me out. When I came to, we were resting for a short period by the roadside. Some of the Auschwitz girls had dragged me along, half carrying me, sharing out my weight. I had a fractured skull; but there was nobody who could or would do anything about it, so I had to force myself to go on with this splitting pain from my temple to the back of my head.

Cold nights by the roadside took a further toll of our column. Once some of us were lucky enough to squeeze into a pigsty. Lucky pigs, so well off in that warm sty! While in there I slid into some sort of hole, but it was cosy enough in there and I was so tired that I happily went off to sleep where I lay. When my friends hauled me out in the morning it turned out that I had fallen into a manure heap, which certainly didn't improve my general appearance.

One of the best nights was spent in a coal mine. Our group found a chamber with a stone floor and settled in comfortably. None of us cared the least about being covered in black dust the next day. We used snow for washing but it didn't make us very clean; in any case, we were once again overrun by lice and spent our leisure moments killing them.

Late one afternoon a familiar sight appeared. An electrified fence marked the boundaries of another camp, Trautenau. At least we would have a roof over our heads for a change. But nobody seemed to be working there, and general chaos prevailed. Transports were being evacuated one after another. After a quick appraisal we took advantage of the commotion. Several of the girls set about organizing food, and now was the time I felt most grateful to my father for those tiny diamond fillings in my teeth. With one of the diamonds and a gold coin I had smuggled out of *Kanada* I managed to buy two whole loaves of bread. It was tempting to eat as much as I wanted right there and then. But the camp was in such disorder that it was impossible to guess how long we would be there or what rations we might expect, if any. Mother and I might have to make that bread last a long time.

It was just as well I had restrained myself. Only two days later we were issued with two days' bread ration each and one tin of meat to be shared between five people. Then we were sent on our way again, still with no notion of our destination or when we might expect more rations.

The original column of about 10,000 had dwindled to less than a quarter. But in that number our Auschwitz hundred had all so far survived. We tried to keep together as before, but got mixed up with other women as we were taken to a field where a train stood waiting in a siding.

This time there was none of the airless claustrophobia of our journey out of Birkenau. Instead we found ourselves packed into open coal trucks. Our guard marked off a square of floor space with chalk, and settled down in it. The rest of us could not sit down unless we sat on one another's laps. For hours we waited as the weather turned to rain and sleet, then to snow. Soon we were soaked through. We tried to be grateful for the free drinking water we collected in our tin mugs.

At last the train moved off. It was hard to tell which way we were heading. We kept off main lines and travelled only through open country and past little villages. After a few hours the train reversed and we went backwards, skirting a large river which I reckoned must be the Elbe. So we were heading north-west. Our guard wasn't too disagreeable a man, as such men went; but he too had not the slightest idea of where we were going, and after a while settled into long periods of sleep, wrapped in his blankets.

During the night the train moved only in fits and starts, for very short distances at a time. In the terrible cold we huddled together. That same night we had our first experience of an air raid. The attack was obviously aimed at the train. The guards leaped out of the trucks and vanished into ditches beside the track. But they kept their guns aimed our way in case any of us tried to follow suit and leave the train. We were not scared by the bombs. By now there were many of us who would not have minded a direct hit. The only thing that suffered, however, was the track. When morning came the train had to crawl backwards again for several hours.

Half a dozen of us from Auschwitz clung together in the truck. Henia was one of the group, and she and the others had done their own bit of food organizing before leaving Trautenau.Mother and I added what we had to the pool and sat on it to make sure none of the other girls could get at it. At intervals we doled out tiny rations.

Everyone mournfully agreed that walking, whatever its disadvantages, was better than this mode of transport. We were covered in coal dust with no hope of getting out of the truck for a wash or a drink. Or for anything else. Those of us not too weak tried to relieve ourselves by balancing on the edge of the truck, bottoms out, with two friends holding our hands. But many couldn't manage it. The floor became a stinking mess and we just had to put up with it. One consolation was that the guards suffered too; another was the sight of devastated towns by the side of the track and in the middle distance. Such visions of destruction were good for our morale. The days of Germany's dominance were reaching an end. But we, too, were close to the end.

On the third day we recognized places we had seen twenty-four hours before. We must have been travelling in a circle. Our precious bread was giving out and there was no likelihood of any more. The guards had provided themselves with ample supplies, and occasionally one would toss a few handfuls into the centre of his truck to watch the girls fight over it: it was like someone throwing scraps to wild animals just for the fun of it.

More and more were dying. When a guard was sure someone was dead he would heave the body up and pitch it out over the side of the moving truck.

Once when the train stopped in a field we saw a heap of rotting cabbages at the side of the track, food impossible to resist. They tasted good as we chewed them, but the after-effects were disastrous: everyone who had taken a mouthful was hit by sickness and diarrhoea, which greatly added to the mess on the floor.

We had been wandering backwards and forwards for five days and nights, bombed at intervals when our train was mistaken for a military transport. By now most of us were too weak to stand. We just lay on top of one another. Towards evening on the sixth day the train ground to a halt again. This time there was actually a station, whose board identified it as Porta Westfalica. We had certainly covered some miles, all the way from south-east Germany to the north-west, not far from the Dutch border.

'*Alles raus, anstellen!*'

We were glad of the familiar order, though it was difficult to stand up and clamber out of that stinking truck. As usual there was a count of the numbers arriving. We looked back in horror. Of the thousands who had started out with us there were scarcely more than 200 left. Yet when we did our own roll-call we found that all the Auschwitz hundred were present. Our group must be indestructible!

In front of us reared high rocky mountains. As we set off up a steep winding path I began to loathe the woods and slopes I had once been so fond of. After an hour we came to a camp. How marvellous to lie on a bunk, even if it did have to be shared with a few others! Even the camp soup and potatoes were hot and tasted delicious after our long fast. Above all there was water, our first real drink for six days.

The camp was run by Dutch women prisoners, who had apparently not been treated too badly and in turn were not brutal to us. We enquired cautiously about some chimneys one of us had spotted in the distance. It turned out they were not chimneys at all but pillars with a tall historic monument in the middle. Explanation of our fears disgusted the Dutch women: they had never heard of gas chambers, and thought we were quite mad.

Even in this camp, though, with the threat of defeat along every horizon, holy S.S. ritual had to go on. There was still the unavoidable evening *Zählappell*. When it was ended, the resident S.S. came to look us over and sort us out for various duties. Mother was lucky enough to be selected for the kitchens. Apart from a few on similar camp duties, the rest of us were marched outside next day, off into a wilderness of rock and woodland. Perhaps we were going to have to hump stones or chop down trees. There had to be some devious programme in the minds of these Germans still clinging to their sacred routine.

After two hours' climbing we began to descend and soon came to a proper road. At the end of it was a huge entrance cut into the solid rock. The noise inside was deafening. We were in an ammunition plant built into the hillside, so well camouflaged that it is doubtful if the Allies ever knew it existed. Machines were going full blast, echoing out of every shaft and tunnel. We couldn't help feeling depressed: once again we would be forced to make ammunition for our enemies.

Lifts took us down into the depths. Ventilation was so poor that after some time you became terribly drowsy. But at least my job took only five minutes to learn and required very little physical effort. I never had an inkling of exactly what I was helping to make, and could only hope it turned out to be a dud anyway.

Germans in the underground factory, a subsidiary of Philips, worked six to eight hours a shift. We slave labourers did fourteen hours. Then we had the long plod back to camp. At least the air was clear and crisp, and the route almost entirely downhill. Mother waited for me every night with an extra helping of hot soup. She also smuggled in hot water so that I could have a wash. It took days and days before my skin acquired a reasonable colour, and still it was impossible to get rid of the lice. Yet the morning and evening walks, tiring as they might be, were also in some ways refreshing. We supplemented our diet with acorns and I used to bring back leaves from the forest to be rolled and smoked. Often you got quite a spectacular blaze at the end of these home-made cigarettes.

Now the air raids were almost non-stop. Explosions sounded all the louder for being bounced back off the rocks. Spring was coming slowly, and the Allies must be coming as well, though far too slowly. If only the Germans would run off and leave us here, somehow we would manage to survive.

One day there was excitement among the Dutch prisoners. 'Girls! Machine-gun fire! You know what that means? Liberation. Any day now we'll be liberated.'

Two mornings later we were not taken on our usual march to the ammunition plant. We old-timers guessed what this meant. Our fears were confirmed when the camp commandant issued the evacuation order.

'*Marschbefehl. Alles raus. Anstellen.*'

Same old refrain. Same plodding towards the railway line and the waiting trucks. How far and how long could they go on herding us? The engine pointed east, back to where we had come from. None of the omens was pleasant.

We stood in rows of five, as ever. During the commotion our Auschwitz contingent had been split up among thousands of Dutch girls. Only five of us succeeded in sticking together and making up one row. I thought I could glimpse a handful of the others not too far away, but most of them were nowhere in sight; at least fifty must have been detached from the rest. As the commandant approached for the inevitable counting ceremony, my friend Henia suddenly went wild. She wanted to rejoin the fifty, wherever they were. Often, as one of the privileged prisoners in Auschwitz, she had indulged herself in dramatic gestures and got away with them, even in front of reluctantly admiring S.S. men. Her outbursts must many times have proved useful and helped others as well as herself to win some concessions, but this time she was asking for trouble. Everyone was on edge. No one was in the mood for her outcry. One of the guards swung round, and it was clear he was on the brink of shooting her. I don't remember thinking about it, even for a split second. I just acted. Before she could rant on any further I knocked Henia out and dragged her to one side.

Though I didn't realize it at the moment, this action saved not just her life but possibly the lives of the rest of our little 'family'. Later we learned that nearly all the rest of the Auschwitz girls had been taken off with thousands of others from the camp and mown down by machine-guns in the neighbouring forest. The camp had to be evacuated; there was not enough room on the train for everyone; there was not enough food. The simplest solution was the usual S.S. one. Not until our next stop did we discover how many were missing: only fourteen of our original hundred got down at the little station of Fallersleben.

The town was the home of the DKW car works, but these were now only smouldering ruins. An air raid was in progress and we were hurried into the only remaining section of a factory's ground floor, to find ourselves amidst a crowd of people of all nationalities. S.S. guards drove us down into a basement, explaining that there were air raid shelters down here. At the end of a narrow passage was a bunker with iron doors which looked as if they would be thoroughly airtight when closed. We of the Auschwitz group eyed them with mounting suspicion.

One girl cracked. 'Gas!' she cried. With one accord we turned and struggled our way back through the mob trying to reach the doors. A couple of S.S. men chased after us in amazement. Renia, my friend Henia's sister, grabbed one by the belt. 'You're not going to gas us. All right, shoot us – go ahead – but we're not going in there.' It was a strange sight, this little slip of a girl shaking that fat S.S. officer to and fro.

Now we all began shouting. Speechless, the man waved us into silence and indicated that we should follow him back up to the ground floor. He called other guards into a small office. 'Now,' he said quietly. 'Sit down. Tell us about this gas.'

We all talked at once, interrupting each other. As it all poured out he began to shake his head. The other men in the room looked shattered. I realized that it was not that they disbelieved us; they simply couldn't take it in.

'Very well,' said the officer at last, 'in any future raids you are excused from going into the bunker. But it's only for your own good, you know, to protect you from the bombs.'

We were not concerned with such protection. Several times a day all the inmates of the building had to go down into the shelters except us. We lay on our bunks, singing and laughing even when bombs hit parts of the factory. All the remaining windows were blown out but still we did not move. I suppose we could have walked out quite easily, for there were no guards – they were the first to rush for the basement.

There was no work to be done. The S.S. wandered around like lost sheep. Their methodical lives had been completely disorganized. We at least were enjoying a well-deserved rest. In a neighbouring hall we found the luxury of hot running water and spent most of our day washing out clothes and scrubbing our bodies, trying hard to get rid of the lice once and for all. There were even flush toilets, the first I had seen for years. The only thing we lacked was food. Our daily bread ration was becoming smaller, the midday soup thinner.

Wonderful smells of cooking still came from the S.S. kitchen. During one air raid those of us still above ground decided to organize a raid of our own. The kitchen women had left a large bowl full of grated potatoes, ready for making potato fritters, when the alarm sounded. We made off with the bowl, shared out the raw potato, and got the bowl back to the kitchen before the all-clear went. The S.S. were furious when they discovered what I suppose you might call our ingratitude, but they were more lenient than they would have been if trained in Auschwitz methods.

Still we were not allowed to sit back and wait for the end of the war. One day without warning we were led out of the building. Some girls hid inside toilets and ruins, hoping to escape when everyone had gone. But most of us felt that, the way things were now, it was safer to be in a crowd.

We were herded into cattle trucks again. The doors were bolted, and we stayed in there for hours. Suddenly we were off with a jolt. We travelled some distance, stopped, started again, stopped and backed, went on and then backwards again.

Our destination was Bergen-Belsen camp. We had heard of it before, and our hearts sank when we saw the faces of the old gang – Kramer, Grese, and the rest of them, who must have been sent here from Auschwitz. We knew what to expect from such creatures. But fortunately Belsen was too crowded to take us in. We were marched back to the trucks, joined by many others evacuated from the camp. There were several more long goods trains on the line, in a field many miles from Belsen, indeed miles from anywhere. At first we thought they were waiting empty, but as we drew nearer there were faint whimpers for help. The hideous truth was that trainloads of prisoners had been locked in and left to die.

Before we could react, armed guards and their dogs rushed us towards the vans. We were bundled inside, and in a flash the doors were bolted and nails hammered in. The footsteps of the guards moved off, becoming fainter and fainter. We had been sealed in like the rest to die of starvation and suffocation.

Our van stank of cheese. It was practically airtight, and the walls dripped with condensation. For a time we screamed and banged for help without really believing any would come. As the atmosphere got worse, everyone clawed and fought to get near the floor or a wall in the hope of finding a faint breath of air. Those in the middle fell silent after a while. It was impossible to tell how many had died or were close to death. I got down on the floor and found a crack between two boards, with the hint of fresh air through the pungent reek of cheese. Somewhere in one of our raids I had acquired a small knife, and with this I started picking away at the crack until I had widened it slightly. Mother and I took it in turns to press our noses to the tiny opening. Yet why bother? It was quicker to suffocate than to starve.

Occasional cries for help grew fewer. Now there was a murmur of groaning, a bout of weeping in one corner which died away, to be taken up in another corner. I listened to the moans of the dying and reproached myself for not having had the courage to give up the struggle long ago. Others had had the guts to throw themselves on the fence. I envied them their eternal peace. Here I was waiting for a slow and terrible end. I touched my head and arms. I was wringing wet from perspiration, and growing drowsy. Every minute felt like hours. I worked out muzzily that a whole night must have passed.

Suddenly there were footsteps. Three or four people coming closer. We summoned up what energy we had left and began to bang loudly on the side of the van. There was an answering knock from the other side. We begged them to hurry, before it was too late.

There was a mumble of voices, and then we heard the bolts slam back. But still it seemed to take hours before the door was finally opened: it was quite a job, getting the nails out. Daylight blinded us. I fell out, and others pushed out over me. We were gasping for air. Not food, for once: just great lungfuls of fresh air.

There were actually only two men there, S.S. guards, looking startled at what they had let loose. Ours was the only truck they tackled. Not a sound came from the others. Everybody must be dead by now. The guards had no idea what to do with the living. They must have realized there was no way of getting us back into that truck. We outnumbered them, and we had no intention of climbing back in again.

One girl said: 'Are you going to let us go?'

The two men studied us warily.

'We're not going back in the truck.' Several shouts confirmed this. 'Either let us loose,' said another girl, 'or take us into a camp.'

It was crazy. We were actually begging to be allowed into the comforts of another concentration camp.

'There must be a camp somewhere near.'

As long as we didn't go back to Belsen.

The guards conferred. One of them knew of a camp a few hours away. He would go to see the commandant and ask if we could be let in. So there we were, waiting for ages until he returned, in the charge of one apprehensive S.S. man. But it would have been hopeless to run off. In our filthy, dilapidated condition we would have been spotted at once, and even at this stage no German would have risked his neck by sheltering a runaway prisoner.

The news brought back by our guard's colleague was that a small camp outside Salzwedel was prepared to admit us.

Summoning up our last reserves of strength we marched away in fives from that train as briskly as we could manage. After some hours we came to the little town of Salzwedel, and a very pretty sight it was: roads, pavements, trim houses and shops, when for weeks we had seen nothing but a wilderness. On the outskirts was the fenced area of a camp, nearer to civilization than most.

So here we were, a few survivors of Auschwitz and other prisons, volunteering to enter yet another concentration camp!

10

Liberation

SOME GIRLS already in the camp were employed in Salzwedel sugar
refinery, but there were no further vacancies and precious little else for
the rest of us to do. They looked quite fit and supplemented their diet
with sugar smuggled into the camp and hoarded in their bunks. We
newcomers had to be content with camp soup.

Then the soup gave out. There was no more bread. Our only food
consisted of raw beet thrown down in an untidy heap, as if we were
pigs. You grabbed what you could. There were rumours that the whole
area was surrounded by Allied armies, so at least we couldn't be
driven on yet again: there was nowhere left for them to chase us. Only
force of habit kept the German routine ticking over.

On the other side of the electrified fence were the S.S. stores.
Through the windows we could see row upon row of neatly stacked
golden-brown loaves and all kinds of tins. And from the S.S. kitchen
came a tantalizing smell of cooking. Our own food would not keep us
alive much longer. It was unthinkable that we should die when rescue
was so near.

The girls who had been here before us still had their sugar to fall
back on, but had no intention of sharing it with us. One night five of
us decided we had suffered enough. It was hateful to stoop so low as to
steal from fellow prisoners, which I had managed to avoid doing all
these years. But it must be done if we were going to survive.

Three of us crept out on our bellies one night and crawled along
beside the walls of the huts. Then somebody stumbled and slipped as
she was getting up, and the girls woke up. But we were not going to
turn back. We plunged right in and dragged the mattresses off some of
the bunks. The inmates of the hut fought and after a wild scrimmage

we were driven off; but I was able to grab some sugar and so did several of the others before we retreated.

In the second week of April work parties ceased leaving the camp for work in the refinery. S.S. guards tossed a last helping of rotting beets and swedes into the centre of the camp and disappeared.

On the morning of Friday 13 April three of us were propped wearily against the wall of our hut talking when a shell exploded above us and splinters spattered all around. Several girls nearby were wounded by fragments, and there was blood everywhere.

I stared through the electrified fence at the S.S. stores. All that food, and so close – if only we could get at it! We were growing weaker by the hour. But none of us dared touch the fence to see if the current was still on. And how did we know there were not still a few S.S. in hiding, waiting for us to make a move before emerging to beat us up?

In the evening a shower of scribbled notes fluttered down on our heads. They came from French prisoners of war, who must have been liberated from a neighbouring camp during the fighting around Salzwedel, and warned us that cables were being laid around our camp. The whole area was mined and it looked as if the Germans intended to blow us all up at the last minute. The French promised they would do their best to cut the electrified fence and cables during the coming night so that we could all escape.

That night the suspense was unbearable. We heard no sound from outside; and no one risked going near the fence to see if the current had really been cut off. A bewildered S.S. man strayed back into the camp next morning. I don't think he himself knew why he had returned. A mob of girls descended on him and tore his uniform to shreds. I glimpsed a dagger under his coat, and was determined to have it. He broke loose at last; but not before I had grabbed it. After that I settled down to go on staring, hypnotized, at the S.S. stores through the fence.

Somebody was shaking me. 'Look! For goodness' sake look, over there, outside the gate. Can't you see?'

A military convoy was rumbling down the road. More S.S. coming back to end it all?

'Those uniforms!' one of the girls was crying. 'Those helmets, they're not German. Never seen those before.'

Suddenly we knew. They were American uniforms.

At first the passing troops appeared not even to have noticed us, but when we began to scream and wave, a couple of tanks turned in our direction. The gates were smashed open. The men flinched from the kisses of the ecstatic, filthy, stinking girls who tried to swarm all over them.

I had only one thought. The current was off. I climbed through the fence, made for the S.S. hut, and smashed its window. My arms were loaded with gorgeous loaves of bread when the rest of the women realized what had happened and came jostling in after me. By the time I fought my way outside I had only one loaf. Mother and I didn't ration ourselves this time. We tore the whole loaf apart and ate until our jaws ached.

We had thought we were too weak to move. But now the prison gates were open, and the town of Salzwedel was wide open, too. Some girls had already rushed off there. I had to follow: for years I had dreamed of the moment when I could at last get my own back. I had the dagger. There would be a use for it.

The five of us who had raided the sugar hoard ganged up again and set off to raid the town, joined on the way by hundreds of men from a neighbouring camp occupied by non-German forced labourers. They were in the same mood as we were, and it was no mood to respect white flags and white sheets hanging from every window.

The four other girls and I hammered on the door of the first house that took our fancy. 'Open up! Come on, open up.' When there was no reply we heaved against the door until it burst open. It was amazing what energy we had now.

On the ground floor and first floor the expensively furnished rooms were deserted. Just as we were about to give up the search we heard a child crying. Running downstairs, we found an improvised air-raid shelter in the basement. In the semi-darkness I could make out a huddle of people in one corner: an elderly man and woman, a younger woman, and two little girls.

'Kill them,' my friends were screaming. 'Go on, kill them.'

I gripped the knife and moved towards them.

The little girl was howling with terror. As I got used to the gloom in the basement I found that looking into her eyes was no different from looking into the eyes of doomed children in Auschwitz. But this one was German.

'What are you waiting for?' one of my friends demanded.

All at once I knew I couldn't throw the knife or drive it into any of these people. If I committed murder, the S.S. would have succeeded. They would have made me like them. All these years my mind had disobeyed everything they tried to inflict on it. I couldn't let them win now. Someone from behind tried to grab the dagger. I clutched it more tightly. Then I threw it as hard as I could away from the petrified family, deep into a door. I sank to the floor, sobbing.

'It's no good, I can't do it. I just can't, do you hear?'

The rest of them backed out of the room. Not one tried to pull the dagger from the woodwork.

Gratefully the older woman tried to shake my hand. She was asking if I wanted anything, anything at all.

I hadn't killed. But that didn't mean they were going to get off scot-free. I told her that I simply wanted to smash up everything in the house.

There was already a terrible racket coming from the first floor. When I got up there I found the others smashing windows and pictures with pickaxes they had somehow got their hands on. I fetched a box of matches from the bathroom and set fire to carpets in room after room. Opening drawers of nice clothes, I tipped the contents on the floor and set fire to them. The only items I actually took away from the place were groceries such as jam, flour and bottled fruit, and a woollen blanket for my mother. In the next house along the road we turned on all the taps and flooded it.

Now the problem was to get the food we had acquired back to the camp. There wasn't a handcart to be found. Finally we broke loose a bathtub, hauled it out into the street, and dragged it from house to house until it was full. It was hard to recognize some of the girls who came out of those front doors: lots of them had thrown aside their rags and clogs, and looked transformed in new outfits they had organized.

Mother was outside the camp gates when I got back, being interviewed by American newspapermen. She was hoarse from talking about Auschwitz. Her story was, I think, one of the first to be released to the world press.

That first night of freedom I couldn't sleep. I kept thinking it was all just a dream and wanted to run outside to see if the Americans were still there. Perhaps they had begun to lose ground and the Germans would soon be back.

As soon as dawn came most of us were off into Salzwedel again. Today I took my time, wanting to look round and see what German homes were really like. I tried what it felt like to lie in a real bed with sheets and pillows. I walked on carpets. In one house, stretching out on the bed, I felt something hard under the mattress. When I drew it out I found it was a large framed portrait of Hitler. The elderly woman of the house, who had been following my every move, trembling, let out a cry.

'Take anything, but please not the picture of my beloved *Führer*, please . . .'

I was in a rage. 'How dare you say that to me?'

Two of my friends came into the room and held her while I smashed the gilded frame, ripped the picture out, and set fire to it. We smashed everything else we could lay our hands on, and carried on through the town, rummaging through cellars to unearth anything the Germans had tried to hide. In one street we came to a dairy with enormous milk churns which we overturned, flooding the place with milk and drinking from cupped hands as we splashed about in it.

The rampage through Salzwedel lasted three days. Then there was a change which took some getting used to. Military governors in all sectors had to supervise the switch from war to peace. What was permissible in the immediate aftermath of the fighting was now illegal. One day it had been a patriotic duty for Poles and others to revenge themselves on their enemy by looting, smashing, and killing; the next, it became a criminal offence.

Notices went up on houses in the town forbidding anyone to enter. Vengeance must now be sought in more orderly fashion. A few days after the liberation I was taken with an American squad to tour surrounding districts in the hope of identifying men and women they wanted to interview. In houses here and there we found S.S. wearing civilian clothes; but often in a corner or even folded over their arms, as though they couldn't bear to be parted from the joys of office, would be coats and jackets in colours I recognized. I asked permission to take a coat from one of the S.S. women, and the Americans let me have it. One S.S. man recognized by another of our girls was brought to the camp and given the job of carrying corpses from the sick bay: there were still many deaths, mostly from dysentery and typhus.

The Americans provided us with a very special treat. We were guests of honour at the ceremonial burning down of the entire concentration camp; and the sight of those smouldering wooden shacks finally convinced me that the days of horror were really gone for ever.

Mother and I at once found work with the Americans. My English was not up to her standard, but I understood enough to make myself useful. Close to what has since become the frontier between East and West Germany, one of my first tasks was to translate haltingly between senior American and Russian officers as they carved up the territory into spheres of influence.

When it was decided that Salzwedel was to belong in the Russian zone, we begged the Americans to take us with them as they pulled out. We left with their first convoy, and found ourselves accommodated in a camp at Brunswick. By now we few Auschwitz survivors were fed up with camps. One of the girls found an empty room in a house, and we all moved in. Yet again food was our main preoccupation. We had no money, and the shops were bare. The Americans came to our rescue by sharing their rations with us and bringing sackfuls of cigarettes. The cigarettes were far superior to those I had made from old leaves and scraps of paper, but I didn't smoke them: they were too valuable as currency, just about the only currency of any worth in Germany in those days.

The region then became part of the British zone, and Mother and I were soon translating for the British military administration. At long last we could live in comfort. A German family were moved into one room in the loft of their attractive villa, and we were given the rest. A car fetched us in the mornings and drove us back at night. We translated confidential documents and statements, and also travelled about a great deal, interpreting at military courts and at interviews with the *Bürgomeisters* of about sixty small towns and villages in the Brunswick region.

A lot of our work was connected with the trials of liberated Poles, who made a habit of sneaking out of their Displaced Persons camps to supplement their rations illegally from German farms, sometimes dragging whole carcasses back to their quarters. It was difficult for me not to show where my sympathies lay. Also there were Poles who had to be persuaded to go home. Many of them were already having doubts about the political situation there. Others, to be frank, seemed in no hurry to rejoin their wives or husbands.

In addition, we helped in identification of S.S. men and concentration camp staff when they had been tracked down or somehow given themselves away. And one day we heard that Hössler had been arrested and was coming up for trial somewhere near Lüneburg. It was he who had responded to my mother's plea and freed me from *Kanada* to travel with her. I would not have been alive today but for him. We knew he had committed many brutalities in Auschwitz, but we owed him a lot and felt someone ought to speak up for him. Mother and I were granted a short leave of absence, and hurried off.

We got very little co-operation. Nobody had invited us to come and nobody was in a welcoming mood. We explained that we had been in the camp and knew of Hössler's crimes, but also knew of some good he had done. We wanted only to give simple, straightforward evidence in his defence. It was not allowed. Everything had been arranged for the hearing and no one was anxious to listen to our side of the story at this stage. So Hössler was hanged.

One member of the Auschwitz S.S. was luckier. Our old stores supervisor, Wünsch, was put on trial in due course at Frankfurt. The Hungarian girl he had been so fond of miraculously showed up and spoke so fervently on his behalf that our '*Wiener Schnitzel*' was acquitted.

Most of the girls in our group were growing weary of staying among the Germans. Mother and I hated living in one of their houses, comfortable as it was – hated the sight of them and were often unhappy at our part in prosecuting Displaced Persons who raided German property. We were in effect defending Germans against our own people who had suffered so much in German hands.

My friend Henia heard of a D.P. camp on a former military aerodrome, run by a Quaker relief team. She and her sister decided to move in there. It was basically meant to be a Polish repatriation centre. Mother and I were asked if we, too, would go there: they urgently needed translators, since none of the Quakers running it had more than a smattering of other languages. Also, my mother would be useful, teaching English to adult classes. Other girls were leaving for Stuttgart, and only seven of us remained from the original Auschwitz lot. We decided to move.

Broitzem camp, misguidedly known as Gipsy when it was inherited from the Americans, was the largest in the British zone. Accommodation was cramped, food and fuel were limited. Some inmates had lost all initiative and any real will to work after years of slavery in Germany. The Quakers sought to restore their pride and redevelop their skills. I was set to allocate jobs in the cobblers' and tailors' workshops. In this latter I had my S.S. coat altered to fit me. Although we had taken it from a woman, it turned out to be a man's coat. After all this time I distinctly remember (the silly things one does remember!) that they had to reverse the buttons for me.

I was sent on a three-week Welfare Training Course, and had further advice in the camp from the man I was to grow so fond of – a personal education as well as a social one. Also I worked long hours in the registration office tracing lost members of families in the hope of reuniting them. Naturally Mother and I used every resource to find out what had happened to our own family. For three months I spent my off-duty periods hitch-hiking between French, American and British zones, between D.P. camps and Red Cross offices, trying to trace some vestige of our old community. I wanted to go back to Bielsko itself, but my mother was upset by the idea of my venturing into the Soviet sector.

All our efforts seemed in vain. Then news began gradually to filter through. We received a letter from Tarnow in southern Poland, near where my father had lodged and worked under his assumed name. The peasant with whom he lived had gone to a lot of trouble to trace us via Lublin, and now told us the sad truth. Somehow my father had been brought to the attention of the Gestapo. He was taken out of the village and shot through the head, after which his body was thrown over a cliff.

My brother Robert was caught crossing the U.S.S.R. in the hope of reaching China and, ultimately, England. He was conscripted into a Polish unit of the Red Army commanded by, of all people, a friend from Bielsko. This Major, whose name was Conrad, told us of Robert's last minutes. They had been dug in for days in the defence of Stalingrad, and Robert, by now a Lieutenant, longed for a drink from a nearby pond. He slid towards it on his belly and was hit by a sniper's bullet and died instantly.

Grandmother, whom we'd had to leave in Zabia Wola, had been taken from there to her death in Belzec concentration camp.

Bit by bit we pieced together fragments of information. Of our immediate relatives, thirty had perished. It began to seem that Mother and I were the sole survivors of what had been a large local family. Our home had been looted and ransacked: we had nothing and no one to go back to.

The only good news we eventually had was that Cousin Max and Lucy had managed to get through. After their dash across the frozen river Bug they had reached Russia, but when they made their identities known they were transported to Siberia. After the war ended, Max returned to Poland to make enquiries about the family, but then for some reason went to Egypt, from where at last we received a letter. He went on via France to the United States, and I know that he later became director of a large company but died at a comparatively early age. It was his brother, who had settled in America before the war, who helped him get there and also vouched for my mother and myself when we were granted special entry permits. But by then I had been working closely for months on end with that very special man in the relief team. He was the one who brought me to life and taught me new things about life, and he was the one I wanted to follow. So, because of him and because of my mother's reliance on her Birmingham relatives, we went to England.

11

Displaced Persons

WHEN RALPH and I married he was being paid, a very small wage by
a boss who nevertheless appreciated his abilities and promised in due
course to take him into the business. Unfortunately the owner died and
the firm was sold off. Ralph went to work with a friend, a German
Jewish refugee who had built up a prosperous upholstery trade during
the war. He too paid Ralph poorly, on the grounds that if he paid the
true value for Ralph's skill the other employees would be jealous.

The local Jewish community made one contribution towards our
wedding. A red carpet had been laid in the synagogue for a more
fashionable wedding just before ours, and it was graciously agreed
that this should be left down for our own ceremony without charge.
The International Centre let us have a room for the reception, and after
our honeymoon we settled into our tiny attic. It was my first real home
since childhood. Even though we had to share one toilet and bathroom
with sixteen other tenants, we thought it was marvellous.

Even with my living-out allowance on top of Ralph's meagre earnings we had scarcely enough to eat after paying the rent. Also I had to
find a little money to help my mother. Suffering from high blood
pressure and no longer capable of doing a regular job, she decided to
go to London and stay with the same friends she had lodged with in
1911. Nowadays few people can truthfully say they haven't a penny in
the world and can't make ends meet; there are all kinds of supplementary benefits to ease really desperate problems. But at that time
such things were unknown to us. We had a roof over our heads, even
if it did constantly let in the rain, so that we had to have a series of
bowls and buckets to catch the drips, but that was about all.

Because of a recession in the upholstery business Ralph was put on short time. He rarely worked more than three days a week and got no pay for the remaining days. But when Dr Brailsford set me up in a full-time hospital job I began to get a regular salary, just enough for us to buy a few pieces of furniture on hire purchase. When a room fell vacant on the floor below, we brought Mother back from London. I approached my uncle to ask if he could possibly contribute some help towards supporting her: he was not too cheerful about it, but in the end did offer £1 a week.

We stayed in that leaky flat for four years, scraping along somehow. More and more I longed for a little house. In what limited spare time I had I wandered the streets looking for somewhere within our means. Mortgages were difficult. Raising a deposit would be difficult. Was nothing ever going to be easy?

At the end of a year in the Orthopaedic Hospital I asked if I might leave. I felt I needed more general experience and was keen to learn the most demanding work – with children. It was a specially difficult branch of radiography, and if I could learn to handle that I would certainly be capable of tackling any other branch. Dr Brailsford was upset at first; but then he saw my point, and was as ungrudging as ever in his encouragement.

Working in the children's teaching hospital gave me another incentive. I wanted children of my own, and a house fit to bring them up in. Children of my own, to carry on the Jewish race. Not in any religious sense: after Auschwitz I retained no belief in a loving God. Some survivors claim that their faith helped them to get through. To me such faith seemed to make little difference one way or the other. I saw people praying while being beaten up, and there was no sign that the prayers helped very much. I saw people kneeling in prayer before being shot or gassed. After you have listened, day after day and month after month, to the screams of children being gassed, smashed or burnt to death, you find it hard to believe that any faith in a benevolent God could be of value. And if it is preached that they are now in heaven and all is well, I still cannot accept that the road to heaven should involve such pain and degradation and terror to the innocent. From time to time I went to the synagogue, but found it meant nothing. Yet I longed to produce Jewish children to make up, in however small a way, for so many who had been exterminated. And I longed to lose the awful feeling of homelessness which I experienced in Birmingham more acutely than anywhere else, even at the worst of times.

After walking endlessly through Birmingham suburbs, I came across just the sort of little house that would suit us. It was in Quinton, in one of those very streets I remembered from that lonely Christmas. We simply had to have it.

It was impossible to get a mortgage on Ralph's earnings alone, and the company I approached would offer a joint mortgage only if I assured them I had no intention of having a family. In fact I was already pregnant with our first child but luckily it didn't show. What I could honestly tell them was that I intended to go on working for years, and they need have no fear of the regular repayments failing. Still we needed a deposit. It came from Jane, one of the dearest of my Quaker friends from the D.P. camp, now living in London. We arranged to pay her back in small amounts each month, like the mortgage. So it was settled. When, later, our second son was on the way, Jane generously waived the outstanding balance as a present.

Mother moved in with us and from then on looked after the house, cooked, and in due course looked after the children. I worked until three weeks before David was born in 1953 and went back immediately afterwards, doing sessions at awkward hours to fit in with feeding the baby. A baby, a dependent mother, a mortgage – and a husband on short time! During the winter we rarely had enough coal to heat the house, and precious little food. I decided that things couldn't get any worse, so let's have another baby now and get it over with.

But for a time things did get worse. Ralph now had so little regular work through his employer that something really had to be done. I urged him to find some opening for himself. Eventually, taking the kids along in the pram – the baby Peter inside and David perched on one end – I went knocking on the doors of small hotels in search of odd jobs. We soon collected quite a few. With no transport of our own, Ralph had to walk to the job and do it on the spot; there was no way of bringing furniture home, except for smaller items which could be pushed to and fro on the pram.

Although we had no car we had a garage. Ralph set up his own little workshop. When we could afford to print a batch of advertising cards I went round pushing them through doors. Ralph soon had enough work to occupy his three empty days. But now his friend turned awkward.

'As long as you're working for me, you ought to bring in any jobs you pick up, not do them yourself.'

It was essential to make a clean break.

I got myself a job in private practice with a radiologist, and fitted hospital sessions into evenings and weekends. This way I could arrange my working hours so that I was free at certain times of the day to help establish Ralph in business. Both the practice and the hospitals were happy, since I was prepared to do those awkward periods which nobody else much cared for, and I got double pay over weekends.

We needed one sizeable long-term commission to make the break possible. Suddenly I was struck by the number of pubs in our neighbourhood, virtually one on every corner. Surely they needed regular repairs to their benches, chairs and that sort of thing? I took the two boys, grown to push-chair size by now, and went to see a director of Ansell's brewery. He was taken back by the sight of this odd creature with her two small children, but heard me out with the greatest interest and agreed to let Ralph put in a quote. As a starter he got an order to re-upholster forty pubs. We found a larger workshop above a garage, and Ralph set up there, though of course most of the work had to be done on pub premises, and he often carried out repairs under somewhat chaotic conditions. But Ansell's proved very pleasant to deal with, and after their merger with Mitchell and Butler continued to put a lot of work Ralph's way.

It was a different story with another big company, which almost crippled us quite early on. Ralph produced a great deal for their chain of shops, turning down other offers so that he could concentrate on this line, until the owner was declared bankrupt and couldn't pay up. (He nevertheless shifted enough money to enable himself to go on living in an attractively wooded suburb of Birmingham, close to where we live today.)

I stepped up the campaign, taking photographs of Ralph's work to various companies and winning orders which gave more scope for his craftsmanship. Among these was one of the country's major groups, with a famous name whose bearer nowadays makes much of his philanthropy. Two directors rolled up one morning and looked, bemused, at Ralph's little workshop. They were impressed by his skill, and returned for another inspection. Eventually they placed a firm order: so many suites in so many weeks at such and such a price, and no dealing with any competitor. This meant a monopoly of Ralph's work until they tired and could squeeze a tighter deal elsewhere. And the price they quoted left no margin whatsoever for us to live on.

Once more in my life I found myself grasping a knife. It was one of the tools from Ralph's bench which I grabbed, not threatening the men, but offering them the handle.

'Why not cut our throats right away while you're at it? Isn't anybody else but you allowed to earn a living?'

We didn't get the contract. On their terms we would not have wanted it.

I have had plenty of opportunity to learn how many long-established

firms with famous names profit from slave labour. The more prosperous they are, the more they demand from those who do the real
creative work, and for a smaller fee. Just as the S.S. would demand so
many gold rings from ghetto inhabitants, in default of which you
would be sentenced to hard labour and ultimate extermination, so
there are great organizations in the so-called free world demanding
your soul and life-blood in return for the most meagre rations they
dare offer – thereby blandly consigning you to ultimate extinction.

I still see the features and routines of Auschwitz everywhere. Everyone I have met since the war slots in my mind into an Auschwitz
setting. I know within a few minutes who they would have been and
how they would have behaved, especially when the chips were down.
There may not be the same undisguised physical brutality in our
contemporary surroundings, but the pattern is the same: personal
viciousness, greed for power, love of manipulation and humiliation.
How do men get and hold the most coveted jobs in big firms? By
starting as 'trusties' and trampling over others on their way to the top.
From *Unterkapo* to *Kapo* to *Oberkapo*, from squad N.C.O. to camp
executive and even higher if you're ruthless enough. You may even be
privileged to eat with the S.S. and use their washroom if you're truly
dedicated to the cause.

When a company offers the public some breathtaking bargains, those
bargains are at the expense of somebody else's breath; never at the
expense of the *Obersturmbannführer's* pocket. In a concentration camp
the conflict would be an immediate battle over one hunk of bread. In
the office skyscraper it is on a longer-term basis: steady attrition,
covered by a veneer of artificial politeness. Nobody gets physically
beaten up, tortured or murdered, but often there is what you might call
a slow campaign against life. This breed of killers prefers scheming in
an atmosphere of polite treachery rather than speaking malice out loud.
But the greed, malice and power lust are at the heart of it just the same.

I had done enough slave labour for one lifetime. But after telling one
lot of exploiters to clear off, what came next?

What in fact came next was the first trickle of German compensation
for my mother and myself. In the late 1950s we received all kinds of
forms to fill in. There were affidavits to be sworn to, questions to be
answered. We needed witnesses to vouch for our wartime experiences,
and these were difficult to locate. Lawyers prepared documents and
required exact details: what had we once owned in Poland, what had
we lost, what damage had our health sustained during the war, what
family deprivations could we establish?

At last money began to appear, some in outright payments and some

in pension form. Mother and I got about £750 each for the imprisonment we had undergone, precisely calculated at so much for each
month of our captivity – so many months in Auschwitz, so many
working in factories, and so on. Later my mother got an extra allowance for her loss of earnings as a qualified teacher and for the loss of
her husband, as well as a widow's pension.

My own compensation came later and was much less. The Germans
took their time, but at least their conscientious attempt to set right
their past wrongs went some way to conciliating the survivors. Still
there was one thing I found hard to forgive. I was never reimbursed
for my loss of education. Their excuse was that I had not attended a
German school and therefore it was not their responsibility. German
refugees who had fled to England before the war and had all the
advantages of English schooling were granted up to a couple of
thousand pounds each for their loss of German education. But a Polish
girl deprived of any education at all by the German invasion of her
country was entitled to nothing.

Neither of us received anything for the house in Bielsko. Those who
had lost their homes in Germany were fully compensated. Not Poles.
A small arbitrary assessment was made for the contents, but since the
house itself was now behind the Iron Curtain there was no way to do
anything about it.

With my own first compensation I insisted on buying a car to
transport chairs and other items Ralph was working on. I also went
round shops with a sample of his craftsmanship in the boot to show to
buyers. Ralph still deals with people we contacted years ago, and no
longer needs to advertise.

Mother's reparation came too late for her to enjoy it to the full. She
was by now in her seventies and in failing health. But she determined
not to waste a moment. Part of her compensation was a one-month
treatment every year at a spa, all expenses paid by the Germans. This
was when she started travelling to Germany. Like her, I went there as
soon as possible, though I was more interested in ski-ing and talking
to people than in taking cures – unless you could describe all that
talking and questioning as a cure in itself, which perhaps it was. One
lump sum of several thousand pounds came to Mother as back pension.
She insisted on our taking this to buy whatever we needed for the
house or Ralph's workshop. She had already bought furniture and all
sorts of odd items for us, and was always adamant on sharing everything that came to her.

My idea was that we should acquire shop premises with a window to
display Ralph's goods, maybe live over the shop, build a bigger work-

shop at the back, and take on staff – someone to look after the shop, and a full-time rep. Ralph was far from keen on such expansion, and preferred to go on plying his trade as he had done before. So what should we do with the money?

We would buy a new house, with more room for the boys to study. And I would study with them. This became an essential theme in our lives. Having now established myself as a freelance radiographer, with considerable freedom in my choice of working hours, I was able to spend time with David and Peter and to educate myself along with them. I got copies of their school books for myself and tried to stay always one jump ahead. Their teachers did not altogether approve of the fact that in this way, learning together as we did, the boys were soon far ahead of their schoolfellows and the syllabus. I am afraid I must have been a dreadful martinet. When David and Peter got home some afternoons and gleefully announced there was no homework today, I dashed their hopes by saying *I* would provide the homework: we would sit down and do it together. Television was permitted only from Friday evening to Sunday.

David grew so used to this discipline that years later when he was on vacation from university and I told him to stop swotting and relax – 'Do go and watch television for an hour or two' – he laughed and reproached me, 'All those years you made me work, and now I've got the habit so badly I can't stop.'

They both got the habit. David became school captain, won a Rhodes Scholarship, and in 1976 qualified in medicine at Birmingham Medical School. In 1978 Peter obtained an honours degree in physics at Manchester University.

As another part of their education, I insisted on taking them to Germany as soon as we could afford it. We camped among German and Austrian holidaymakers so that our boys could mix with them and get along with them.

In our new home, as in the little one in Quinton, I still had my mother to talk to. We sometimes argued and quarrelled, and the children wondered what on earth was going on. Often Ralph got along with her better than I did. But we had this bond which was beyond anyone else's understanding. We knew things they had never known, things we didn't have to endure any longer, but when suddenly it was essential to talk to *someone* about the past, even if only for a few minutes, we had each other. We never wallowed in self-pity. There was no need. The only need was to speak for a while; and we spoke the same language.

Only one other person ever showed any real interest in the subject.

While we were still in the Quinton house and I was X-raying patients at Dudley Road Hospital, the receptionist was an American girl, Nancie Beg, whose husband was on a twelve-month scientific research project in Birmingham. Nancie became a very good friend, and was the first to ask real questions about my experiences. A mere fifteen years had gone by since the end of the war, but she had heard little of such things and was spellbound.

'You've simply got to get that down on paper,' she urged. 'You've just got to write a book, before it's all forgotten.'

I already had more than enough to do, trying to help Ralph and bringing up the boys while working what are now referred to as 'unsocial' hours. But in between casualty work, with drunks staggering in and emergencies descending on us at unpredictable intervals, I used the occasional lulls to scribble furiously and get it out of my system. My English was still limited when it came to the written word, so I kept everything short and straightforward. I have been told that in some way this made the story all the more compelling. I don't know about that, but I do know the writing of it was good for me. *I Am Alive* came out in 1961. It was a short book and no best-seller; and still there were so many people who simply did not want to know. They were not ready for it, didn't want to read about such unpleasantness, didn't want to admit to the truth. It was all over, wasn't it? If it had ever happened at all . . .

I always felt that the story ought to be told at greater length and set in the proper context. At the time it served mainly as a sort of purging of my own personal lingering angers and fears. There was still so much left unsaid. Now I believe I can see it all in a truer perspective than I could have hoped to do then. The return trip to Auschwitz set the seal on it.

Mother, last of our Bielsko family apart from myself, died in 1974, taking her memories of marriage and happiness and then of the extermination camps with her. My own family's schooldays and university days are past. And David is grown up – and beside me now, here and now, in Auschwitz.

12

Return to Auschwitz

You see grass. But I don't see any grass. I see mud, just a sea of mud. And you think it's cold? With your four or five layers of clothing on a bright crisp day like this, you feel the cold? Well, imagine people here or out beyond that fence working when it snowed, when it rained, when it was hot or cold, with one layer of clothing. The same layer and no change of clothing unless you were a skilled organizer. And you couldn't take those stinking rags off or they'd be stolen immediately.

Look at me daring to walk along the *Lagerstrasse*. In my day you were not supposed even to set foot on it, let alone walk along it. I close my eyes and there they are, those women, *Kapos* and the rest of them, strutting up and down. It was forbidden for scum like me to venture near the edge of that trench or peer down into it.

I open my eyes, and there's nobody. Open my eyes and see grass. Close my eyes and see mud.

Here it is, the gate between two sections of the camp which I had to get through to visit my mother. And there are the electrified fences. Don't go too close. The watch-towers still look down. There must still be guns in there, trained on you.

I belong here. I knew I ought never to have come back, because it has proved I've never been away. The past I see is more real than the tidy pretence they have put in its place. The noises are as loud as they ever were: the screams, the shouts, the curses, the lash of whips and thud of truncheons, the ravening dogs. Here was where I received my personal education. This is my old school. Education sticks with you for the rest of your life. Whatever curriculum and discipline other people may cling to or rebel against from their schooldays, here is where my standards were established: to obey or try not to obey, to revolt against or slyly circumvent, and always, either way, to fear; standards which, no matter how distorted, can never be forgotten.

I walk on grass which was once interminable mud. Beneath the green surface the ground is still muddy. My feet sink in. It's not so much spongy as just that little bit wetter so that it squelches and threatens to suck you down and trap you there, so that you breathe faster and want to drag your feet out and escape before it's too late.

Imagine it (I can't imagine it any other way) with 100,000 people trudging through that mud, hear the plopping sound of wrenching your clog out of the mess until maybe you no longer had the strength to wrench it out . . .

In another thirty or forty years there will no longer be people like me alive, no one who can actually say, 'I've watched with my own eyes one, two, three million people go to their death.' I would like you, David, to be able to testify that your mother was here and you've been here with me, and tell your children what I've told you and shown you, so that it will never be completely erased from history. I've had thirty good years. But most of the rest of my relatives, my grandmothers and aunts and my father's family and my mother's, and my school friends, were robbed of those years. The ashes of more than thirty of my relations could well be in this very place. Yet there are new cheats and liars and schemers writing that it never happened and couldn't ever have been true. So I must reply in these pages that it *was* true.

All a myth? Come and see for yourself.

I'm trying to locate Camp BI. It all looks so alien. With so many of the huts pulled down or fallen down, I can't get my bearings. Some of the stone huts are still intact, but the wooden ones have disintegrated, leaving an odd pattern of little brick chimneys and heating channels jutting up all over the place. But this stone building must be part of BI. Look at it. And just look over there. When I close my eyes again I see camps, nothing but camps. This one we're standing in was one of the smallest. Beyond it stretched the streets and terraces and factories of a city of slaves as far as the eye could see.

There's the railway line I helped to build, over there. Not that I actually laid the rails: I dug ditches and carried cement. That's why my hands aren't ladylike. And there's where they often turned the dogs loose on you.

Here. This is Block 20, one of the first of my huts. This door is where the *Blockälteste* stood, and where the bread ration was doled out. Every time you went in you were issued with your bread ration,

usually with a savage blow as well. And inside . . . come in and have a
look . . . oh, yes, I often bought myself a place to sleep on one of those
boards. Bought it with crumbs of bread, because if you didn't you were
liable to end up on the floor. Look at the mud on that floor and
imagine it. Look at the end of the hut, too. That's where the bucket
was. Just one bucket, and you couldn't use it most of the time so you
lay in your own mess and everyone else's mess. No water, only miserable scraps of food, and you were beaten all the time . . . how long do
you think *you* would want to go on living?

Here's the little room of the *Blockälteste*. Here she kept her roll-call
book, and here she slept, and here she had her own little stove to keep
her warm.

Outside, the 'meadow' is green with grass. That's something I
simply can't get used to. It was never like that when we stood for hours
waiting for roll-call numbers to match up. Never like that when
women collapsed and died in the mud or froze to death on the hard
winter ground.

Another block, and what's this? A washroom actually attached to
the hut. I never got as far as that in my Auschwitz career. Water was
something you won only by bartering bread – if you could organize
the surplus bread in the first place. You couldn't take it away in a
container, so had to bribe your way into some place where there was a
tap, however miserable and polluted its trickle might be. I can hear it
now, the negotiating and auctioning.

'I've got a bowl of water. You can have it for two spoons of sugar.'

'I haven't got two spoons. Tell you what – I can manage one spoon,
and a little bit of bread.'

'Here.' Another girl pushes her way in. 'If she doesn't want it, *I'll*
give you two spoons of sugar for it.'

As for the official issue of drink, since liberation I have confirmed
what many of us suspected at the time. Soup and so-called tea or
coffee (the distinction was hazy) both had poison added. Prisoners
working in the kitchens were supervised by S.S. women who regularly
measured out a certain quantity of white powder into whatever the
liquid might be. We assumed it was some sort of bromide but had no
way of discovering anything about its properties. I recently learned
that a Polish doctor is currently engaged in research into the poison,
which is called Avo. It contributed to the revolting smell of the soup,
but you drank the stuff because you were desperate. And if you had no
other food, you were in trouble.

In the hospital compound there was an abundance of *Lagersuppe*
because few of the sick could swallow their full ration. Prisoners on the

staff lived on the leftovers. Mother had a lot of it before she noticed the effect it was having. Drink too much, and you couldn't think clearly all day. It gave you diarrhoea, slowed down other physical movements, and left you totally confused. I am sure now it contributed to the degeneration of those who became *Muselmen*; and was probably a factor, along with psychological shock and malnutrition, in women ceasing to menstruate.

Only when you progressed to the status of a more privileged prisoner and no longer had to rely on the camp soup and tea could you hope to recover from their effects, which must have been deliberately calculated to depress the majority of the inmates.

All through this existence ran the three necessities which I have already emphasized: food, sleep, and shit. And along with these went one necessary implement. Your bowl. I remember my bowl in Auschwitz was a red one. If you didn't have your bowl you didn't get your soup. If you didn't have your bowl you didn't have your toilet. And how did you wash the bowl out before you ate again? You didn't. Or you washed it with your own urine.

Here's the toilet block. That came rather late on. Even then there were thousands of women trying to get in before roll-call. And no paper? You mean toilet paper? You must be joking.

Over here . . . this huge cart. Now, I haven't thought of that for years. It used to be dragged into the camp loaded with bread rations, drawn by male Russian prisoners-of-war, the few survivors of the 20,000 exterminated just before our arrival in Auschwitz. Once the bread had been distributed, the cart came in handy for removing corpses which lay by the roadside and outside every block.

Oh, God. This is the hospital compound. The very place where I had to help load Hanka and Genia on to the lorries. Load my own friends on just when they were on their way to recovery from illness. That finished me. Really finished me mentally. Everybody went that day. Everybody. Only my mother stopped me going with them or on to the fence.

Mother saved my life then and on so many occasions. We couldn't have survived without each other. There was no way of struggling through all on your own. You had to have somebody helping you, and you had to help somebody else; without some such bond there was nothing to cling to. I don't know much about the men's camp other than what I have since read in books such as the detailed and deeply moving Ota Kraus and Erich Kulka document, *The Death Factory* (and reading it can never be the same as living it for oneself), but those authors and others admit that conditions in the women's camp of

Birkenau were many times worse than those the men had to suffer.

Down here is the *Kanada* enclosure. Pretending to be a factory with a nice lawn outside. I close my eyes and at once the air is filled with screams; and when I open them I think that *this* is the dream, for the building isn't there, and there are no longer any chimneys for the smoke to pour out of.

We're walking through the birch wood now. There's the pond behind what used to be one of the crematoria. Yes, I'm getting my bearings, I can work out where it stood. And the sauna – look, that's still here, the very same one I remember. And I'm going to scratch my name and number and dates into the wall. I've never disfigured a monument before, but this time I've just got to leave a record behind, to go along with my Auschwitz record which they must still have somewhere filed away in the camp archives.

The path along which our *Kapo* led us has to be here somewhere. So much is overgrown, but it must be here.

People from the whole of Europe were brought to this graveyard. Just remember, that's what it is: a vast graveyard. I'm looking for the white house, but I can't find a trace. Over there, across this clearing, maybe? Walking through these woods, that small group of us on our visits to the main camp, we saw ... yes, here are the foundations. So that's all there is left? All that's left save for the echoes, the steady bup-bup-bup of pistols firing into the back of people's necks.

The ground's a different colour over here. Must be some pits or something. We climb up this mound, and on the other side ... that grey patch ... you know what that is? I dig in with a stick, and up come sodden ashes and a piece of bone.

'Yes,' says David. As a doctor he has no doubts. 'This is human bone.'

A tiny morsel of one of the millions who perished here.

Let's invite those people who say it never happened, invite them here and ask them to explain these ashes and fragments of human bone. And the empty gas canisters they keep in Auschwitz museum – if there were no gassings, where did all those canisters come from and what were they used for? My eyes didn't play me false. I saw just that sort of container being tipped into the vent. And I heard the sounds that followed.

So many were exterminated that you had to numb yourself against any reaction. As long as there was a sea of people, death was too vast to comprehend. But acts of individual brutality still scream in my mind. A mother might be trying to pacify her child as she began to fear the worst, and then because of some other upset the S.S. would cease the pretence of calm and orderliness. An S.S. man might come and tear the child away, pick it up by its head or legs and just smash it to death in front of the mother. It was something never to be forgiven. Mother and child were condemned to death anyway: could they not be allowed to go to it quietly together? Even if there had been any impersonal logic behind the German extermination programme, even if they genuinely felt their basic policy was a stern moral necessity, then at least they could have let people go to their ordained death with dignity rather than under the torment of gratuitous brutality.

If instead of those unknown Germans in Salzwedel I had met one of the S.S. men while the dagger was still in my hand, would I have used it? I'm pretty sure I would. And I'd have had no guilty conscience afterwards.

Some death camp survivors don't want to remember, either because the pain is too great or because there are things of which they are ashamed. A lot of prisoners did not behave as honourably as they ought to have done, and perhaps survived just because of that shabby behaviour, while others died as a result. Free now, they are the ones who feel most guilty and least ready to talk about their experiences. In Israel after the war a number of Jewish *Kapos* were brought to trial for what they had inflicted on their own people. I have watched girls get themselves into positions of authority and then set about beating up their friends. In the outside world they have dozens of reasons for not wishing to remember. And dozens of reasons for not wishing to run across anyone else who has survived and might remember *them*.

And my own legacy from the camp? I'm not ashamed of anything I did there and not ashamed to be alive today. Like many of the girls, I looked for good work groups where we did nobody any harm and stood the chance of helping others. No, I have no lingering guilt. But I do bear other marks. Recurrent bouts of thrombo-phlebitis remind me of my beating in Auschwitz. The whip carved a hole in my thigh which has left a permanent scar. Other blows fell on my spine and left me with recurrent back trouble. Then there's a mark on my arm where one of the S.S. dogs was set on me. And I'm still walking around with a hole in my head! The fracture in my skull from the blow of a rifle butt during the death march occurred in one of the few places, I have since been told by a specialist, where it would do no lasting damage; but I still have a deep cleft there, very sensitive to the touch.

In spite of this inheritance I love to exercise – out of defiance rather than as therapy. A few acquaintances regard me as a bit of a freak because I'm always on the go, seeking new challenges. I swim and run and do my daily stint on an exercise bicycle, and I still love to go ski-ing. I'm forever trying to prove something to myself. The physical exercise is often quite unpleasant. I do some first thing in the morning when I certainly don't feel in the mood for it, and I set myself nearly impossible objectives: 'Today I must do a hundred knee bends,' I say to myself, 'and then tomorrow I'll do two hundred if it kills me.' I swim a mile feeling what a boring thing it is to do; but I've proved to myself that I have the self-discipline.

Loneliness is something I've rarely experienced apart from that dismal early period in Birmingham, when I was truly alone in a crowd of indifferent strangers. Most of my life there have been people around me whether I wanted them or not. Thousands in the extermination camp; crowds in the D.P. camp; a constant coming and going in the hospitals and nurses' homes. Even when at last we had our own house, my mother was always around, Ralph was often working at home, and I had to share my time between patients, family, and my husband's business. You would have thought that after the stifling years of over-crowded imprisonment I'd have wanted to be on my own when the chance arose. But I had got so used to having people about me.

Indeed, what I missed most for some time after the war, improbable as it sounds, was the sort of friendship I had known in Auschwitz. I hadn't realized, until I lacked them, just how strong those bonds between staunch friends had been. In our little 'families' we were more direct and more honest than in most relationships you find in the out-side world. In Auschwitz everything was clear-cut, one thing or the other. There was no veil of politeness or deceit. The S.S. might try their deceptions, might be forever trying to confuse you and cheat you, but somehow you found a way of resisting. You had your enemies and you had your friends. Somehow those friends are still with me in spirit. If I do anything worth while, it's with their support.

Only since my mother's death in 1974 have I slowly adjusted to the idea of being alone from time to time. Now that David and Peter are grown up and have left home, it is something I'd have had to cope with anyway. But even now I need to be doing something. I feel I'm living on borrowed time. Into each day I have to pack all the lost oppor-tunities and energies of those lost youthful years. Throughout that time I existed only for the immediate day, not knowing if there would be a next one. Coming out into the world it was hard to grasp that there was now not just a today but a tomorrow as well, and there were going to be tomorrows beyond that – a next week, a next month . . . So there had to be projects worth pushing into the future. That is why I can't help setting myself so many tasks and targets.

There was Ralph's business as well as my own radiography. With

some of the money my mother passed on I eventually bought a couple
of houses to do up and let at low rents to students needing accommodation, perhaps with some vague thought about my own schooldays
that never were. One of them showed his gratitude by absconding with
all the furniture. But I've persevered. Then, travelling on the Continent,
I noticed openings which British exporters were missing, and couldn't
bear to see such opportunities neglected. I established profitable
contacts for a firm of Scottish tartan manufacturers, none of whose
sales representatives had bothered to learn any foreign language, and
took only a small commission on my successes. The successes were so
considerable, however, that I was politely dismissed once the whole
operation was running smoothly and told that the firm was setting up
its own European agency.

   I would like to devote more of my time to setting up in this country a
worthy memorial to the victims of the Holocaust. The Simon Wiesenthal
Centre in Los Angeles and the new Holocaust Library and Research
Centre in San Francisco could serve as a model. I envisage a permanent
museum with reference material and visual displays, helping to educate
teachers so that they in turn will use their knowledge in schools. Not to
nourish hatred but to preserve the truth. There has been the most
appalling indifference towards the Holocaust over the last thirty-five
years. The full story of that calculated genocide hardly ever features in
history teaching, general studies, or classroom discussion. Only
recently has there been an awakening of genuine interest. The majority
of letters flooding in after my television appearance came from members
of the younger generation, anxious to know more and wondering why
they had so far been given so little information.

   Perhaps the Allies, like the camp toadies, have too much to be
ashamed of. They would rather not reopen their old files for the world
to see. We know they were given full evidence of the extermination
programme in Auschwitz very early on. Photographs of columns heading into the gas chambers were smuggled out and reached both Britain
and America. In April 1944 two Slovaks managed to escape and sent a
full account of life in Birkenau to the Allies, including a copy to the
President of the United States. No attention was paid. It was easier to
tell oneself that it couldn't be true than to cope with the full impli-
cations of the truth.

   The democratic countries didn't want to listen. They must listen now.
Those of us who survived have a duty to those who died. They are not
here to speak: we must speak for them. But time is running out. I am
one of the youngest survivors, and I am committed for the rest of my
days to spreading the truth. It is important to combat the mounting

propaganda of lies which could lead to another wave of Nazism in Europe and even in America. Another Holocaust. And just as dangerous is sheer indifference – the indifference of civilized countries before the war, during the war, and now. Oh, all that concentration camp stuff, we've heard it all, there's been too much fuss, what's it got to do with *us*?

'It's over and done with.' I've heard that said so many times. 'Anyway, it could only have happened in Germany.'

That's not true. It could have happened anywhere. It can still happen anywhere if conditions are right. There are awful signs, in fact, of it beginning to happen in various parts of the world yet again, and getting worse. Young Germans today should not be burdened with their fathers' and grandfathers' guilt. But they should learn from the Holocaust and ensure they have no cause for guilt over their future behaviour. And that is true of others: France, for example, and England. When you hear someone speak slightingly of 'That Jewish lot down the road' or rant 'It's high time those bloody blacks were rounded up and sent back where they belong', you are listening to the very people whose prejudices can so readily be inflamed by cunning propaganda at the right moment. And, just as guilty as their predecessors in Hitler's day, there will be those who take no active part, yet allow it all to happen through selfish indifference.

At present the Poles look after the remains of Auschwitz admirably. I am slightly perturbed by their emphasis on national resistance and the massacre of Poles and political prisoners rather than the much vaster Jewish extermination programme. But there are difficulties. The S.S. managed to destroy most of Birkenau before leaving, while Auschwitz I remained almost intact. Parties cannot be taken round what is left of Birkenau as often as round the patriotic exhibits in Auschwitz I. Nevertheless I was impressed by the number of visitors not only from countries in the Eastern bloc but from Holland, Belgium, even Japan (none from the United Kingdom), and even more by the dedication of old inmates who have returned voluntarily to the scene of their most tragic years in order to act as guides, tell the story as it really was, and work in the archives and library. Let those who deny the existence of such places come with me and walk round. And if four million Jews were not exterminated in Auschwitz–Birkenau, where are those four million now? Six million in all, in Europe.

There is one question above all which younger people ask, and to which their elders have still provided no satisfactory answer. Quite apart from the evasions of those who hoped to avoid war with Germany, who played their devious political games, who had their own antipathies and anti-Semitic spites, how could the Germans themselves contemplate such a campaign of mass murder and persist with it right up to the last minute? One man's perverse hatreds may be, if not forgivable, at any rate comprehensible. The ambitions of sycophants and bully boys hoping to climb on the bandwagon are also easily explainable. But that the whole weight of a national régime should be flung fanatically behind a programme of genocide defies all understanding. It was not just one wild, destructive outburst such as can happen during fierce battles or in immediately vengeful reprisals; it was a steady campaign of cold-blooded savagery which lasted over several years.

Even if you try to set aside all normal human emotions and decide to rationalize it entirely from the Nazis' own basic premise, you find that it still doesn't hold up. Why, if they were so proud of their attempt to 'cleanse' society of the Jews, did they go to such lengths to keep details of the Final Solution secret? Ought they not to have boasted to the world of their achievement? And if their aim within the concentration camps was to subdue the inmates by a reign of terror, how could the full force of that terror be exerted if even the mention of gas chambers and crematoria was forbidden? The whole world, Hitler declared more than once, would be grateful to him in the end. Yet the end was camouflaged, and the means were hushed up.

Then, when the war was so obviously close to being lost, instead of putting every effort into defending the homeland the S.S. intensified the slaughter of Jews. Much-needed trains were filled with them, thousands of troops who could have been at the front were employed rounding them up and escorting them, and right at the end the trains and men were still being wasted in transferring prisoners from one camp to another. Even the profits made by the S.S. from the exploitation of slave labour, and even the use of *Volksdeutschen* and *Kapos* in much of the administration, could not by then justify the drain on military resources.

Whichever way you look at it, the whole thing was crazy. It was as though the Nazis were possessed by a mental disease so progressively malignant that it excluded all logic and was beyond any cure.

It has been said that to understand all is to forgive all. Perhaps one reason why the Nazis can never be forgiven is that their obsessive evil can never be understood.

While being interviewed for the television programme which took me back to Auschwitz I said something which later sounded strange to my own ears. I declared that I thought the experience had been worth while. This was not at all what I meant. No such horror and such slaughter of innocents could ever in any sense have been worth while. What I was trying to convey, and what I say now, is that if such a terrible thing had to happen, or was allowed by human negligence and human wickedness to happen, then personally I would sooner have gone through it than not gone through it. But I would not wish that anyone in the world should ever have to suffer such agonies again.

Index